Too many books on discipleship have unreasonable expectations for a pastor, let alone an entire church. *Discipleship Today* contains a Biblical methodology driven by exegesis of the Scriptures. Dr. Burggraff shows how the entire church can all work in this process, from the pulpit to the small group to the individual mentor.

Michael J. Matiscik
Pastor, Christian Fellowship Church
Hammond, IN

At the heart of Jesus' final instructions to his followers lies the profound concept of discipleship. Yet many question the church's success in fulfilling this core mission. In this accessible book, Burggraff beckons the church to return to her central purpose—developing true disciples of Christ. *Discipleship Today* is a call to action. It challenges readers to embrace the principles of discipleship, transforming their lives and the lives of those around them."

Timothy E. Miller, Ph.D.
VP of Academics, Dean of Faculty
Shepherds Theological Seminary

If you were to ask ten Christians today what it means to make a disciple, or what discipleship is, you might receive ten different answers! Bringing together biblical truth, historical data, and pastoral wisdom, Andrew T. Burggraff skillfully navigates his readers through the terrain of biblical discipleship, equipping Christians today to faithfully carry out Christ's command.

Jesse Randolph
Pastor-Teacher, Indian Hills Community Church
Lincoln, NE

Discipleship Today

Discipleship Today

Applying Biblical Discipleship in Today's Context

Andrew T. Burggraff, Ed.D., M.Div.

SHEPHERDS PRESS

Cary, North Carolina

To my parents, Dave and Lucy,
who instilled in me a love for God and His Word.
&
To my wife, Delecia,
and our children, Andrew, Anna, Aaron, Brody, and Tanner.
I love you!

Contents

Chapter 1

The Current State
of Discipleship

I F YOU WERE TO provide a letter grade for how well the church is discipling believers, what letter grade would you give? I have asked that question of numerous seminary students, pastors, church leaders, and members of congregations. I can't remember a time that the letter grade that was given was an A or A+. Typically, the response that is given is that individuals would rate discipleship in the church somewhere around a C or D. Now, this rating is for the church collectively. I know that many individual churches are faithful, dedicated, and intentional in making disciples. However, the church at large is not doing a good job at obeying the final command that Jesus gave His followers in Matthew 28:19–20, "Go, therefore, and make disciples of all the nations."

How can I make that statement? Recent studies have revealed concerning trends that can be attributed in part to a lack of biblical discipleship. When biblical discipleship is taking place, the results of these studies would look dramatically different. What are we facing today as a church? What does the research tell us about the current state of the church and discipleship?

Decline of a Biblical Worldview

A recent survey of the worldview of Americans conducted by the Cultural Research Center at Arizona Christian University shows that "although seven out of ten consider themselves to be Christian, just 6% actually possess a biblical worldview."[1] Len Munsil, ACU President, defines a biblical worldview as follows: "A biblical worldview says 'love your neighbor' and brings hope, joy, faith and prayer to any trial or any crisis."[2] Though you may or may not agree with his definition of a biblical worldview, it is important to understand the stark contrast between self-professing Christians and their mindsets regarding others and their handling of trials.

Other key findings from the 2020 survey:

- Only one-fifth of those attending evangelical Protestant churches (21%) have a biblical worldview.

- The number of American adults holding a Biblical worldview has declined by 50% over the past quarter century.

- Regarding the next generation, the numbers are even more startling. A mere 2% of those 18 to 29 years old possess a biblical worldview.[3]

Obviously, the results of this study are concerning. As Dr. Barna explains, "The fact that fewer than one out of five born-again adults hold an actual biblical worldview highlights the extensive decline of core Christian principles in America."[4]

"Why is it dangerous that so few Americans have a biblical worldview?" asked Len Munsil, ACU President. "We see it now with our response to the COVID19 pandemic. Un-like past national crises—including the Great Depression and World Wars—when Americans responded with charity, prayer and hope, today we are seeing widespread hoarding, panic and hopelessness."[5]

Why is the nation experiencing a dramatic decrease of a biblical worldview? Why is the next generation abandoning a biblical mindset? This is a concern for today's church.

Exodus of Individuals from Churches (Especially the Younger Generation)

John Dickerson in his book *The Great Evangelical Recession* examines the exodus of young people from our churches. According to Dickerson's surveys, the evangelical church is losing members at the rate of "2.6 million per decade."[6] He continues to highlight the growing concern that this figure indicates: "If the evangelical church is only about 22 million Americans, as a growing crowd of respected sociologists estimate … then we lost more than 10 percent of our people in the last ten years. That's worth losing sleep over."[7]

Regarding the loss of young people in the church, Dickerson makes this startling statement.

> This may be the most disturbing of all the trends we must face—our failure to retain our own children as disciples. Simply keeping our own kids would hold us steady with population growth. But we are not keeping our kids or holding our percentage in the population. Research indicates that more than half of those born into evangelicalism are leaving the movement in their twenties.[8]

3

David Kinnaman, a lead researcher for The Barna Group, in his book, *You Lost Me: Why Young Christians Are Leaving Church … and Rethinking Faith*, conveys several disturbing statistics about the young generation of Christians in America.

> The ages eighteen to twenty-nine are the black hole of church attendance; this age segment is "missing in action" from most congregations.… Overall, there is a 43 percent drop-off between the teen and early adult years in terms of church engagement. These numbers represent about eight million twentysomethings who were active churchgoers as teenagers but who will no longer be particularly engaged in a church by their thirtieth birthday.[9]

Kinnaman continues to describe the exodus of young adults from the church by presenting the research conducted by The Barna Group:

> In one of Barna Group's most recent studies, conducted in early 2011, we asked a nationwide random sample of young adults with a Christian background to describe their journey of faith.… The research confirmed what we had already been piecing together from other data: 59 percent of young people with a Christian background report that they had or have "dropped out of attending church, after going regularly." A majority (57 percent) say they are less active in church today compared to when they were age fifteen. Nearly two-fifths (38 percent) say they have gone through a period when they significantly doubted their faith. Another one-third (32 percent) describe a period when they felt like rejecting their parents' faith.[10]

It is not only the young evangelicals who are leaving the church. In a 2009 study by The Barna Group, adults with children in the home are leaving the church as well.

> Demographics suggest that the mainline churches may be on the precipice of a period of decline unless remedial steps are taken. For instance, in the past decade there has been a 22% drop in the percentage of adults attending mainline congregations who have children under the age of 18 living in their home.[11]

These trends indicate that a growing number of evangelicals, especially younger evangelicals, are leaving the church. This exodus reveals an area of concern as to how the church is discipling believers. Why are we losing so many of our young people? Why are believers leaving the church and abandoning a biblical worldview?

Lack of Bible Knowledge

Bible knowledge is the byproduct of Bible reading. One cannot know the Scriptures without reading and studying the Scriptures. Sadly, studies reveal that many people who fill the pews of our churches do not read God's Word on a regular—much less daily—basis.

George Guthrie, a professor at Union University, acknowledges confounding research regarding Bible reading among believers:

> In a recent survey by LifeWay Research, the No. 1 predictor of spiritual maturity among church goers was whether or not they read the Bible on a daily basis. Yet, only 16 out of 100 of those who regularly attend our churches read the Bible every day; another 32 percent read the Bible at least once per week.

This means that more than 50 percent of people who come through our doors on a regular basis only read their Bibles occasionally, perhaps one or two times per month, if at all. Even more sobering, only 37 percent of those who attend church regularly say that reading and studying the Bible has made a significant difference in the way they live their lives. Only 37 percent.[12]

In addition, George Barna has made the following statement based upon his research findings regarding Bible reading and subsequent spiritual growth from the reading:

Bible reading has become the religious equivalent of sound-bite journalism. When people read from the Bible, they typically open it, read a brief passage without much regard for the context, and consider the primary thought or feeling that the passage provided. If they are comfortable with it, they accept it; otherwise, they deem it interesting but irrelevant to their life, and move on. There is shockingly little growth evident in people's understanding of the fundamental themes of the Scriptures and amazingly little interest in deepening their knowledge and application of biblical principles.[13]

A startling fact from Barna's research is that those individuals who read the Bible spend little time allowing the truths of Scripture to impact their lives.

A recent study by the Barna Group highlighted the decrease of Bible reading during the national pandemic. While the pandemic eliminated various time distractions with a lockdown, the number of people that read Scripture decreased drastically. David Roach cited the following in Christianity Today from the Barna research:

> Between early 2019 and 2020, the percentage of US adults who say they use the Bible daily dropped from 14 percent to 9 percent, according to the State of the Bible 2020 report released today by the Barna Group and the American Bible Society (ABS). A decrease of 5 percentage points in a single year was unprecedented in the annual survey's 10-year history; between 2011 and 2019, daily Bible readers had basically held steady at an average of 13.7 percent of the population.[14]

With a decrease in Bible reading, it would appear obvious that there is a decrease in biblical literacy because individuals do not know the contents of Scripture. They are not reading God's Word.

Research has shown that the church is continuing to witness a recurrent lack of literacy among believers. Stephen Prothero states the following regarding America as "A Nation of Biblical Illiterates":

> Evangelical pollsters have lamented for some time the disparity between Americans' veneration of the Bible and their understanding of it, painting a picture of a nation that believes God has spoken in Scripture but can't be bothered to listen to what God has to say.... According to recent polls, most American adults cannot name one of the four Gospels, and many high school seniors think Sodom and Gomorrah were husband and wife.[15]

In 2010, one of the six "megathemes" for American churches as listed by The Barna Group was that "the church is becoming less theologically literate." The results of various surveys led George Barna to state, "The data suggests that biblical literacy is likely to decline significantly."[16] Stephen Marlin summarizes several surveys to reveal how bad the trend of biblical illiteracy has become:

- Many professing Christians cannot identify more than two or three of the disciples
- 60 percent of Americans can't name even five of the Ten Commandments
- 82 percent of Americans believe the phrase, "God helps those who help themselves" is a Bible verse
- 12 percent of adults believe that Joan of Arc was Noah's wife
- A considerable number of respondents to one poll indicated that the Sermon on the Mount was preached by Billy Graham. (This old saint has been around a while, but not that long!)[17]

Albert Mohler, after examining various surveys related to biblical illiteracy, states the following about the source of the biblical literacy problem in America:

> Christians who lack biblical knowledge are the products of churches that marginalize biblical knowledge. Bible teaching now often accounts for only a diminishing fraction of the local congregation's time and attention. The move to small group ministry has certainly increased opportunities for fellowship, but many of these groups never get beyond superficial Bible study. Youth ministries are asked to fix problems, provide entertainment, and keep kids busy. How many local-church youth programs actually produce substantial Bible knowledge in young people? Even the pulpit has been sidelined in many congregations. Preaching has taken a back seat to other concerns in corporate worship. The centrality of biblical preaching

to the formation of disciples is lost, and Christian ignorance leads to Christian indolence and worse. This really is our problem, and it is up to this generation of Christians to reverse course.[18]

Mohler provides a challenging reminder that biblical knowledge is a critical component in the discipleship and spiritual growth of an individual. If churches marginalize Bible knowledge, they will be filled with believers who have superficial knowledge of God's Word.

Due to the lack of Biblical literacy, basic truths from Scripture are overlooked and subsequently unlearned. Sadly, many believers do not even realize how little Scripture they know. George Barna made the following statement regarding believer's lack of recognition as to the Bible's impact in their lives:

> The problem facing the Christian Church is not that people lack a complete set of beliefs; the problem is that they have a full slate of beliefs in mind, which they think are consistent with biblical teachings, and they are neither open to being proven wrong nor to learning new insights. Our research suggests that this challenge initially emerges in the late adolescent or early teenage years. By the time most Americans reach the age of 13 or 14, they think they pretty much know everything of value the Bible has to teach and they are no longer interested in learning more scriptural content. It requires increasingly concise, creative, reinforced, and personally relevant efforts to penetrate people's minds with new or more accurate insights into genuinely biblical principles.[19]

Similar research led Craig Keener to make the following statement regarding the state of the church in relationship to the importance of Scripture:

> At least in the United States, the church has lost much of its emphasis on teaching Scripture. Most things are driven by marketing; while marketing can be a useful tool, it is not a criterion of truth or morality. Some messages are more popular than others because they are more marketable to consumers. Many churches across the theological spectrum succumb to the culture's values, whether its sexual mores or its materialism; many churches fight for their tradition, or focus on charismatic speakers' experiences. Yet most of the western church today neglects the very Scriptures that we claim to be our arbiter of truth and a living expression of God's voice.[20]

Keener presents a significant concern for the church. Churches today de-emphasize the Scriptures and as a result many believers are biblically illiterate.

The Christian church is witnessing a lack of biblical literacy in the lives of believers today. The statistics are staggering as to the lack of biblical knowledge that most believers possess regarding basic biblical truths. How can one be a true follower (disciple) of the Savior if he does not know Christ's message and instruction? Why do believers fail to read God's Word on a regular basis? Why is there a lack of passion for the truths contained with the Bible?

De-Emphasis of Discipleship Training

In addition to the above concerns, a final concern is the de-emphasis of discipleship within churches. Noted leaders have made claims as to the lack of discipleship occurring within the church. This lack of emphasis on discipleship is not a new phenomenon. James Montgomery Boice, a noted Bible expositor, voiced many years ago a concern about the deficiency of discipleship within the church:

> There is a fatal defect in the life of Christ's church ... a lack of true discipleship. Discipleship means forsaking everything to follow Christ. But for many of today's supposed Christians—perhaps the majority—it is the case that while there is much talk about Christ and even much furious activity, there is actually very little following of Christ Himself.[21]

More recently, George Barna made the following statement after an extensive interview process with Christian adults: "Not one of the adults we interviewed said that their goal in life was to be a committed follower of Jesus Christ or to make disciples."[22] The result of his study led Barna to conclude the following about discipleship: "To pastors and church staff, discipleship is a tired word. To most laypeople, it is a meaningless word. But let's not get hung up on terminology for the moment. Let's get hung up on our failure to produce indefatigable imitators of Christ."[23] Barna challenged our churches not to forsake the importance of discipleship but rather to make discipling others a key component of our church ministries.

"To most laypeople, 'discipleship' is a tired word."

Within the last several years, a team of researchers from LifeWay Research sought to evaluate the discipleship outcomes of churches. After extensive research, they made the following claim, "Since Christ-centered discipleship results in transformation, we can confidently assert that most churches are deficient in discipleship. This is a scathing claim as our entire mission as believers and churches is to 'make disciples.'"[24]

This claim was made after two different surveys were conducted by LifeWay Research in 2008 and 2010. The first study (2008) surveyed seven thousand churches. The second study (2010) was a multi-faceted, mixed-method study which began with an interview of twenty-eight experts in the field of discipleship. This initial interview process was followed by a survey of one thousand Protestant pastors in the United States. Finally, a survey was conducted of four thousand Protestants in North America. After the respective surveys were completed for the 2010 study, the research team would state:

> Sadly, we can make this bold diagnosis based on the far-reaching and sobering research: There is a discipleship deficiency in most churches resulting in a lack of transformation.... The sad reality is that the daily lives, aspirations, and desires of many people in our churches mirror those who do not claim to know Christ.[25]

Why are believers comfortable living like unbelievers in this secular world? Why is discipleship not a priority for the church? Why are believers at ease with living contrary to the Bible's standards?

When taken collectively, these four areas present a dismal picture of the current state of discipleship taking place (or not taking place) within American churches. These concerns ought to arouse an alarm over the loss of understanding and practice of biblically based and historically practiced discipleship. The purpose of this book is to help the reader understand biblical discipleship and apply it in today's context.

Chapter 2
Defining Discipleship Biblically

O VER THE YEARS, I have been asked the question, "What is discipleship?" Oftentimes the question is asked because individuals have heard various definitions of discipleship, complicated characteristics of a disciple maker, numerous misconceptions as to what constitutes the discipleship process, etc.

Before one can accurately discuss what discipleship should look like in our churches and lives today, a proper understanding of what discipleship is and what it was in Jesus' day is critical for the modern disciple maker.

Understanding Discipleship in Jesus' Day

The English term "disciple" is the translation of the Greek word *mathetes* (μαθητης). This noun is used around 260 times in the Gospels and Acts. The term generally refers to an adherent to a philosophy or to a person. It is important to understand the historical development of the term *mathetes* so that we appreciate how Jesus' audience interpreted the meaning in the New Testament.

The Greek term, *mathetes*, means "pupil, learner, disciple."[1] The term "disciple" is not a new concept introduced in

New Testament writings but was used in the Old Testament period as well as in Greek philosophical schools of the classical and koine Greek time periods.[2] The Old Testament records the concept of a disciple as a "learner," "follower," "apprentice," and "beginning scholar."[3]

In Greek culture, the term *mathetes* dates to the time of Herodotus.[4] The term and its derivations were used in the writings of Homer, Xenophanes, Plato, Socrates, Aristotle, Josephus, Philo, and others, and carried a range of meanings such as "apprentice," "follower," "learner," "pupil," "disciple," etc.[5]

This broad range of defining terms is important to note as one seeks to understand the concept of a disciple in Jesus' day. In Greek Culture, a disciple was a committed follower of a great master, philosopher, or religious figure. The commitment assumed the development of a sustained relationship between the follower and the master, and the relationship extended to imitation of the conduct of the master. This is the notion of the word understood by a Greek audience at the time of the writing of the New Testament.[6]

"Disciples," then, were individuals who were committed to a master who provided the philosophy/teaching and pattern of life that they could follow. In the New Testament the term *mathetes* is used to describe the "disciples" of Christ. In the Gospels, Jesus had many disciples. There are the twelve disciples of Jesus in Matthew 10:1–4 and Luke 6:12–16. Jesus commissioned and sent out 70–72 disciples in Luke 10:1. In addition, a large group of disciples are identified in Luke 6:17: "Jesus came down with them and stood on a level place; and there was a large crowd of His disciples, and a great throng of people from all Judea and Jerusalem and the coastal region of Tyre and Sidon."

However, the concept of New Testament discipleship did not strictly apply only to the twelve apostles, the seventy who were sent out, and the crowds that followed Jesus. NT discipleship also involves those individuals who will accept Christ in the future and follow His teachings. Therefore, the construct of a "disciple of Christ" has clear application to 21st-century Christians. The term "disciple" will also include those who in the future enter a saving relationship with Jesus Christ and become a follower of the Savior. David Turner, New Testament scholar, professor, and commentator, describes the New Testament disciple, as well as future disciples, as being characterized by the following: "A disciple is literally one who follows an itinerant master, as have Jesus' disciples. But Jesus will soon depart from this world, and discipleship will take on a more metaphorical meaning. Following Jesus will entail understanding and obeying his teaching."[7]

D. A. Carson, describing the processes of discipleship, states the following:

> To disciple a person to Christ is to bring him into
> the relation of pupil to teacher, "taking his yoke" of
> authoritative instruction (Matt 11:29), accepting what
> he says is true because he says it, and submitting to his
> requirements as right because he makes them. Disciples are those who hear, understand, and obey Jesus'
> teaching (Matt 12:46–50).[8]

Expounding upon this definition of a disciple, Donald Hagner provides an explanation of the concept of discipleship described in Matthew 28:19–20 (The Great Commission):

> The word "disciple" means above all "learner" or
> "pupil." The emphasis in the commission thus falls
> not on the initial proclamation of the gospel but more
> on the arduous task of nurturing into the experience
> of discipleship, an emphasis that is strengthened and
> explained by the instruction "teaching them to keep

all that I have commanded" in v 20a. To be made a disciple in Matthew means above all to follow after righteousness as articulated in the teaching of Jesus.[9]

Disciples as Apprentices

Not only was a disciple a "learner," but he was also an "apprentice" of a teacher. The relationship of disciple to teacher is more than just "student" to "lecturer" and implies an intimate relationship such as "apprentice" to "mentor."

I am often asked, what is the best word to describe a disciple in Jesus' day? The most accurate term that I could use is the idea of an "apprentice." Not only was a disciple a "learner," but he was also an "apprentice" of a teacher.

To illustrate this idea of "apprentice," let me share with you a historical illustration of apprenticeship. The artist Rembrandt is considered one of the greatest artists of all time. For centuries, numerous works were attributed to him. However, due to modern technology and analysis, it has been determined that many works that were once attributed to him were done by his students. Rembrandt's studio in Amsterdam was one of the greatest teaching enterprises but was not the most organized. Many works done by students of Rembrandt became intermingled with Rembrandt's work.

Jori Finkel, describing this intermingling of artwork, states the following:

> For the last three centuries, and especially the last three decades, art historians have been trying to sort out this mess, working to distinguish master from apprentice. By some counts a good three out of four drawings once believed to be by Rembrandt were actually done by his students.[10]

The works by Rembrandt's apprentices so resembled the work of the master that for centuries it was difficult to distinguish between the two. The apprentice learned from, trained under, and ultimately resembled the master.

With this example of apprenticeship in mind, the disciple in Jesus' day was called to resemble and imitate the master. Imitation of the behavior of a human master became a significant feature of a disciple of a teacher. The disciple was so committed to the master that he or she wanted to imitate their conduct. Sometimes, a follower literally mimicked the physical characteristics of the master. However, most of the time, the disciple was so committed to the master that the disciple tried to emulate the overall lifestyle of the master. This relationship moved away from strictly learning from a master to more of a characterization of imitation of conduct.[11]

Defining Disciple and Discipleship

Defining a Disciple

The disciple of Christ is urged, throughout the New Testament Scriptures, to grow in his spiritual life. Once the believer has accepted the gift of salvation, he becomes a new creation. Paul states, "Therefore if anyone is in Christ, he is a new creature; the old things passed away; behold, new things have come" (2 Cor 5:17). Part of the obligation as a new creation is to become more like Jesus. A disciple is a believer in Christ who is becoming "transformed into the likeness of Jesus Christ."[12]

To become a mature follower of Christ, the believer must strive to develop the mind of Christ. In 1 Corinthians 2:16, Paul states the following: "For who has known the mind of the Lord, that he will instruct him? But we have the mind of Christ." The believer needs to live, act, respond, and even think like his Savior. This demands that there is constant transformation of thinking and of one's mindset so that one can become more like Jesus in every aspect of life. Specifically, "a disciple of Jesus is one who has come to Jesus for eternal life, has claimed Jesus as Savior and God, and has embarked upon the life of following Jesus."[13]

A disciple, then, is a *born-again believer who desires to learn what the Bible teaches, seeks to obey God's instruction, is committed to following Christ's example, and teaches the truths of Scripture to others.*

Defining Discipleship

The term "discipleship" may be difficult at times to define. Today, it is being used as a catchall term for anything from mentorship to small-group discussion, from meetings at a coffee house to the title for a conference at a sports arena. However, it is best to understand discipleship as "a deliberate process of moving Christians forward spiritually."[14] Wilkins highlights that "to make disciples" means to help others walk with Jesus in the real world. This includes helping others come to Christ and grow in their relationship with Christ in all areas of life. It means becoming like Christ.[15]

Discipleship has also been explained both as "becoming a complete and competent follower of Jesus Christ" and "the intentional training of people who voluntarily submit to the lordship of Christ and who want to become imitators of Him in every thought, word, and deed."[16] The process of discipleship has been committed to the church, the bride of Christ (Eph 4:4–16). The church is to be involved in the process of transforming the believer from a babe in Christ to a mature follower of Christ (1 Pet 2:2).

Discipleship, then, is *the process of learning the teachings of Scripture, internalizing them to shape one's belief system, and then acting upon them in one's daily life.*

Transition of the Term "Disciple" in the New Testament

As stated previously, the term "disciple" is used roughly 260 times in the Gospels and the book of Acts. The first time the term "disciple" is mentioned in the New Testament is in Matthew 10:24. The last time it is mentioned is in Acts 21:16. The word "disciple" or "disciples" does not appear in the rest of the New Testament. What happened to the term? Did the Great Commission cease being important for Christians? Why doesn't Paul use the term in the Epistles when he himself studied at the feet (was a disciple) of Gamaliel (Acts 22:3)?

The command to "make disciples" given in Matthew 28:19–20 is still as important today as it was when Christ gave the command to His disciples at His ascension. However, the term changed and transitioned to other terms and pictures in the New Testament. As the first century continued, several images and terms seem to have replaced that of disciples following a teacher or sitting at the feet of a rabbi. The terms that replace "disciple" appear to be the following in addition to others:

- *Believers* (Rom 10:4)
- *Christians* (Acts 11:26; 1 Pet 4:16)
- *Mature* (Eph 4:13–15; 1 Cor 2:6)
- *Saints* (1 Cor 1:2; Rom 1:7; Eph 1:1; Col 1:2; Eph 5:3–4; Rev 13:10)

Also, several word pictures began to be used in the New Testament to describe disciples or believers. Believers are described as:

- A *family* with *brothers* and *sisters* (John 1:11–12; Rom 8:14–16; 1 John 2:12–14)
- A *body* with *members* (Eph 1:22–23)
- A *temple* or *building* with *living stones* (1 Cor 3:9–17; 1 Pet 2:4–5)

Thus, though the terms and pictures used for believers transitioned away from that of disciples of a master-teacher, the core concept remained the same. These new word pictures and descriptive terms for disciples foreshadowed the interdependence that individuals would have in their walk with Christ while still dependent upon His teaching and leading. Also, these images pictured a future obligation that disciples would have to one another in the church. The implications of these new word pictures and concepts will be elaborated on in the following chapters.

Chapter 3
Principles of Biblical Discipleship, Part I

A S WE SEEK TO practice discipleship in today's context, it is critical that we understand what biblical discipleship is, what Jesus called us to do and be, and what characteristics should be evident in our lives. The following two chapters are not meant to be a complete examination of all the passages that relate to discipleship principles in the Old and New Testaments. However, several passages will be examined to provide an overall picture of discipleship in the New Testament. Our goal in the next two chapters is to examine what each passage meant to the original audience and to apply that meaning to the modern practice of discipleship.

Matthew 28:19–20
We Are Commanded to Make Disciples (Lifetime Learners)

Go therefore and make disciples of all the nations, baptizing them in the name of the Father and the Son and the Holy Spirit, teaching them to observe all that I

> *commanded you; and lo, I am with you always, even to*
> *the end of the age.*

As one studies the Scriptures related to discipleship, Matthew 28:19–20 is probably the first passage that comes to mind. This passage has been labeled The Great Commission. Jesus commissions His followers one final time as He prepares to ascend to heaven. This commission and final command are to be the passion of their hearts. Likewise, this same commission rings out to us today. Jesus' final command is to be the focus and passion of the church. This command should drive and define our mission as individual disciples and as churches.

Jesus had spent several years training His disciples (making disciples), and now He requires them to make disciples of others. The command that Jesus provides His disciples is to reproduce themselves into the lives of others. They were to take the treasure that Jesus had given to them (His life, teaching, and example) and share that treasure with all nations.

In the last chapter, we examined the definition of a disciple. Without reiterating those details, it is important to remind ourselves of what Jesus was calling His disciples to do. As Jesus called, trained, taught, and invested in them, now they are to do the same with others.

Ulrich Luz explains that The Great Commission in Matthew 28:19–20 involves discipleship beyond the twelve apostles and impacts believers today.

> "Disciples" are not only the twelve disciples of the
> earthly Jesus; Jesus' discipleship occurs at every place
> where his power becomes active among people (v.
> 18b; cf. 9:8; 10:1) and his commandments are kept (v.
> 20a). Therefore, the mission command of the Risen
> One is also transparent for the present. It is directed
> not only to the eleven apostles at the beginning of

church history; the apostles are figures with whom all disciples of Jesus in all times can identify. The mission of the risen Jesus is for them also.[1]

The Nature of the Command

It has often been mistaken that the command in Matthew 28:19 is "go." Many churches, mission groups, and denominations misunderstand the command within Matthew 28 and spend their efforts winning new converts instead of anchoring them in the Christian faith.[2] The command that Jesus gives to His disciples is to "make disciples" of other individuals. Jesus' commission, which is imperative to all His followers, involves one primary command: "make disciples." This command is accompanied by three participles in the Greek: going, baptizing, and teaching.[3]

Jesus' command: Make disciples.

Craig Blomberg provides important insight into the relationship of the command "make disciples" regarding the participles.

> The verb "make disciples" also commands a kind of evangelism that does not stop after someone makes a profession of faith. The truly subordinate participles in v. 19 explain what making disciples involves: "baptizing" them and "teaching" them obedience to all of Jesus' commandments. The first of these will be a once-for-all, decisive initiation into Christian community. The second proves a perennially incomplete, life-long task.[4]

The idea behind the first participle "going" is that it is assumed that disciples will be going out and telling others about Jesus. The participle is unique in that it functions like a verb.[5] Jesus does not need to command us to go and tell; the assumption is that believers are going out and telling unbelievers about the Savior. In other words, the participle could be read, "as you are going." It is just assumed that we would be going to the lost and telling them about the Savior. Grant Osborne describes the force of the participle "go" or "going."

> "Go" is the operative act, as now God's people are no longer to stay in Jerusalem and be a kind of "show 'n' tell" for the nations but they are actively to go and take the message to the nations.[6]

To "make disciples of all nations" does require people to leave their homelands. However, not everyone will be a missionary and take the gospel to unreached parts of the earth. Jesus' focus remains for all believers to duplicate themselves wherever they may be.[7] The activity demanded in the Great Commission is not to "go," but rather to "make disciples." It is critical to note that the command is not to simply evangelize but to perform the broader and deeper task of "discipling" the nations.[8] Jesus previously commissioned the disciples to proclaim the kingdom to Israel alone (Matt 10:5–6; 15:24–27), but now He commands them to disciple all the nations.[9] The commission is not simply to proclaim the good news, but it has the end result in mind, to "make disciples." It is not enough that the nations hear the message; they must also respond with the same wholehearted commitment which was required of those who became disciples of Jesus during his ministry.[10]

The Way Individuals Are Discipled

Jesus stated at the close of Matthew 28:19 that the disciples were to make disciples by "baptizing" and "teaching." The two participles should not be interpreted in the same way as the participle "going." Rather, they should be interpreted as participles of "means" (i.e., the means by which the disciples were to make disciples was to baptize and then to teach).[11] Baptizing and teaching "beautifully describe both the sacramental and experiential sides of discipleship which are essential aspects of ecclesiology."[12]

Baptizing

The first "means" by which new believers are discipled is through baptism. The eleven disciples were to make disciples by proclaiming the truth concerning Jesus. Their hearers were to be evangelized and enlisted as Jesus' followers (i.e., become new disciples). Those who believed were to be baptized in water in the name of the Father and of the Son and of the Holy Spirit. This act would associate a believer with the person of Jesus Christ and with the Triune God.[13]

In biblical Greek, the term "baptize" means "to immerse."[14] Though baptism did not save an individual, it was a critical step in obedience as a follower of Christ. Through baptism, the disciple identified publicly with Jesus Christ. This baptismal practice served as an outward expression of the inward commitment and change that occurred in the life of a believer in Christ.

Jesus, in the Great Commission, makes baptism an essential component of discipleship. The new believer is baptized under the rulership of Christ. Baptism was an act of initiation, and Matthew 28:19 states that disciples initiate others (after salvation) into the church. Baptism was part of Christian practice universally and from the beginning, and it is unlikely that the early Jewish Christians would baptize fellow Jews without some sort of approval from Jesus (cf. John 4:1–2); therefore, a command of Jesus to baptize was important to the eleven disciples.[15]

Baptism would become the key first step that initiates new disciples into the church (which will be established later in Acts 2). This baptism is a single act, distinct from repeated Jewish ritual washings. It is done with the Trinitarian formula invoking the Father, Son, and Holy Spirit, and so it also contrasts from John's baptism (Mark 1:4).[16] Baptism will be a once-for-all, decisive initiation into Christian community.[17]

Teaching

Those who are baptized are to be taught not only to know all of Jesus' commands but also to obey all of them (Matt 28:20).[18] Throughout the book of Matthew, Jesus has functioned as the teacher, but now the disciples are to teach on His behalf (because Jesus is physically leaving the earth). But though the disciples are now to do the teaching, the teacher-disciple relationship is still with Jesus. The disciples are not the ones that the new disciples are to emulate; rather, new Christians are to be imitators/disciples of Jesus.

What the disciples are to teach is what they have been taught by Jesus. As they teach, Jesus will (now in a new way) be present as mentor/model for the new disciple (Matt 28:20b).[19] In Matthew 28:20, the content of the teaching is given to the disciples—"all that I have commanded you." This expression has in mind the teaching of Jesus in the Gospels as it was directed to the disciples. First and foremost, the disciples are to be obedient to what Jesus has commanded them, and then as a by-product of this obedience they are to pass on His teachings to others. The idea of replication is fundamental to Matthew's thought here.[20]

There are two different Greek words which convey the idea of "teaching" in verses 19–20 ("make disciples" v. 19 and "teaching" v. 20). The "teaching" in these two verses seems to include two things:

    (1) Bringing those who are out of Christianity into it: "teach all nations." The word "teach" carries the sense of "make disciples, proselytize them, bringing them over to my religion."

(2) An indoctrinating of those who are brought into the new religion into a practical observance of its holy truths. "Teaching them to observe all that I commanded you" (v. 20).

Once the initiatory work is done (evangelism), this is the work to be pursued (indoctrination). The new believer, having been brought to the faith, is to be taught practically by disciplers how to live by faith.[21] Teaching obedience to all of Jesus' commands forms the heart of disciple-making. If non-Christians are not hearing the gospel and not being challenged to make a decision for Christ, then the church has disobeyed one part of Jesus' commission. If new converts are not faithfully and lovingly nurtured in the whole counsel of God's disclosure, then the church has disobeyed the other part.[22]

Application for Today

Once new believers are initiated, mature disciples must build the new believers into stronger disciples by teaching them Jesus' message. The summaries of Jesus' teachings earlier in Matthew's Gospel (chs. 5–7; 10; 13; 18; 23–25) work well as a discipling manual for young believers.[23] For instance, Jesus says in Matthew 5:3-11 (The Beatitudes) that blessed are the merciful, the pure in heart, the peacemakers, etc. You can help a new believer you are discipling by encouraging him or her to think, "How can I apply this today?" What does it mean to be merciful? What does pure in heart mean for the believer? How can I be a peacemaker in my home, at work, etc. This instruction (discipleship) proves a perennially incomplete, life-long task.[24]

Matthew 28:19–20 provides for the believer a commission to obey the command of Jesus to "make disciples" of all peoples. The requirement of "going" is assumed by Jesus as a byproduct of a saving relationship with Christ. Because Jesus has redeemed you, the assumption is that you will want to tell others about Him. The means by which believers are to "make disciples" is by "baptizing" and "teaching" them. "Baptism" is the introduction into the Christian community while "teaching" involves a lifelong task of becoming more like Jesus Christ.

Luke 6:40
We Are to Resemble the Master in All Areas of Life

A pupil is not above his teacher; but everyone, after he has been fully trained, will be like his teacher.

In Luke 6:40, Jesus provides His disciples with a maxim regarding the relationship between a teacher and his pupils. This passage provides not only an important principle in relation to New Testament discipleship but also a beautiful picture of the relationship that disciples have to the Master Teacher (Jesus Christ).

The Nature of the Teacher-Pupil Instruction

In the Greco-Roman world, the teacher-pupil relationship was a personal one. Before the widespread availability of books, a pupil depended on his teacher's instruction.[25] Because books were not readily available and oral instruction was standard, a student (disciple) virtually lived alongside his teacher.[26] Teachers were regarded as authorities, and the student's role was not simply to get information from the teacher but rather to follow a teacher by adopting his teaching as normative for life.[27] A critical point to understand is that Jesus describes the end result of the disciple's instruction when He states, "after he has been fully trained, he will be like his teacher." The disciple would eventually mimic the teacher's instruction and the instructor himself.

The verb "fully trained" means "restored" (1 Pet 5:10, NIV) or "perfectly united" (1 Cor 1:10, NIV). The term is also used in Mark 1:19 to describe James the son of Zebedee and John his brother "mending the nets." David Garland highlights the implications this term has on discipleship: "Christian discipleship implies mending one's ways."[28] The instruction in the teacher-pupil relationship involves reordering one's personal and spiritual life. Ceslas Spicq writes, "the Christian life involves steady progress in preparation for glory, or the restoration and reordering of whatever is deficient either in one's personal life or in one's relations with one's neighbor."[29] This depth of instruction is not achieved in a one-time sermon series or in a six-week discipleship course. Rather, this instruction requires continuous spiritual formation (Phil 3:12–16).[30]

The Content of the Teacher-Pupil Instruction

In the ancient world, the content of the instruction was critically important within the teacher-pupil relationship. It is often assumed in modern teaching that content should drive the instruction. Modern educational researchers and experts suggest that other factors beyond simply content are involved in the education of an individual. Specifically, the role of the teacher and his/her ability to convey the content of instruction is critical in the education of others. Robert Marzano, a world-renowned educational specialist, states the following: "The conclusion that individual teachers can have a profound influence on student learning even in schools that are relatively ineffective, was noticed in the 1970s when we began to examine effective teaching practices."[31] In a comprehensive research study involving more than 100,000 students from hundreds of schools, the research reveals that the teacher is the significant difference in student achievement rather than content. "The results of this study will document that the most important factor affecting student learning is the teacher.... Effective teachers appear to be effective with students of all achievement levels, regardless of the level of heterogeneity in their classrooms."[32]

In the New Testament time period, the teacher-pupil relationship is assumed to be one in which the teacher not only imparts a body of information (content) but also praxis/practice (to mimic the actions of the teacher).[33] Thomas Hudgins states, "Mere cognition was never the exclusive goal of learning and education in the Old and New Testaments."[34] Rather, education involved taking the cognitive and relating this information to relational aspects of one's life.[35] A key component of the content in the teacher-student relationship was not only a transfer of knowledge from teacher to pupil but also the transmission of experience and the character of the teacher himself. The pupil was not only to learn from the teacher (cognitive), but he was also to imitate the teacher (conduct).[36]

The Goal of the Teacher-Pupil Instruction

The text in Luke 6:40 highlights the goal of discipleship from a Jewish mindset. François Bovon states, "The goal of instruction for a disciple in Judaism consisted in becoming like his or her teacher in order eventually to become a teacher himself or herself."[37] Luke, however, does not expect the disciples to be teachers exactly like Jesus Christ (which is impossible because Jesus is omniscient and holy). However, Luke is encouraging the disciples to strive to be like the Master in their ethical behavior (as a byproduct of gaining spiritual knowledge). Discipleship involves more than intellectual learning; it involves learning that impacts the head, heart, will, and body. Once an individual enters a salvation relationship with Jesus Christ, he then has the power or ability to mimic the Master (through the power of the Holy Spirit).[38]

Application for Today

The point of this passage is not for disciples to make disciples who resemble themselves. Rather, the disciple should ultimately resemble the Master (Jesus Christ). Future disciples are not to become carbon copies of the copies. Rather, through the study of the Scriptures (in conjunction with the teaching of the disciples), they are to resemble the Master, Jesus Christ. Thomas Hudgins explains this relationship: "Jesus becomes the center of an individual's relationship to God, not just salvifically but also instructionally."[39] A disciple must be ready to learn—from human wisdom and wisdom from above.[40]

Though mentors/disciplers today are to provide an example for mentees/disciples to follow, the ultimate goal of discipleship is to point the learners to Christ. The modern day discipler needs to point those whom he/she is discipling past themselves and ultimately to Christ. I do not want those whom I am discipling to resemble me. I want those whom I disciple to resemble Jesus Christ. That is the goal of discipleship. We are to resemble/mimic/imitate the Master. We are to act like the Master in word and in deed. By this action, we reveal that we truly are "Christians" (imitators of Christ).

Luke 14:26–27
We Are to Be Singular in Our Allegiance to Christ No Matter the Cost

If anyone comes to Me, and does not hate his own father and mother and wife and children and brothers and sisters, yes, and even his own life, he cannot be My disciple. Whoever does not carry his own cross and come after Me cannot be My disciple.

There is a huge difference between being involved and being committed. Jesus had a group of followers who were involved. Many of these people followed him because of His teachings, because of the healings, or because He was the Messiah and they believed He would set up His kingdom shortly. People followed Him for several reasons, and Jesus began to teach them that if they were going to be His disciples it would require a lot more. The same is true 2,000 years later. There is a big difference between being a hearer (a casual participant) and being a disciple.

Discipleship demands deep commitment.

The setting for this text was during the time in which large crowds journeyed with Jesus from Galilee to Jerusalem (v. 25). The people mistakenly saw in Jesus an earthly ruler who was marching to Jerusalem to establish His kingdom, and they wanted to be there with Him and His disciples. But in Jerusalem, He would not ascend a throne; He was on His way to die on the cross. Jesus intended to impress on the people their need to examine their commitment to follow Him. These followers would have to count the high cost of discipleship before they made up their minds to throw in their lots with Him.[41]

Human leaders oftentimes take great delight in having the masses follow them. However, Jesus does not accept an insincere following of Him on the part of the crowds. The central truth of this passage is that Jesus wanted to emphasize that the cost of discipleship requires careful consideration. Before such a commitment to Christ is made, one must be willing to deny himself and forsake all to follow Christ.

The section which contains these two verses regarding discipleship is Luke 14:25–35. The purpose of this section of Scripture was for Jesus to explain to His followers the cost of being His disciple. The section begins with an introduction (v. 25), transitions to two parallel sayings on discipleship (vv. 26–

27), continues by providing two parabolic sayings with application regarding discipleship (vv. 28–33), and concludes with a challenge against half-hearted discipleship (vv. 34–35).[42]

The opening sayings (vv. 26–27) and the application (v. 33) express the total commitment required from disciples of Jesus Christ. This pericope describes what it will take to be a disciple of Jesus.[43] The reason Jesus provides the two parables (vv. 28–32) is to provide an illustration of the importance of correct evaluation before venturing into a task (building a tower, v. 28) or large undertaking (war, v. 31). In both examples, it is critical for an individual to "count the cost" before venturing into the task. These illustrations (parables) challenge the individual to consider the cost of discipleship. The disciple of Christ must be willing to pay the cost or else the task will go uncompleted, and he will be considered useless (vv. 34–35).[44]

Jesus challenges those who are following him that there is a cost to being his disciple (vv. 26–27, 33). In verses 26–27, Jesus makes two challenging statements related to the cost of discipleship. It is critically important to understand what these two statements mean so that one can understand the true cost of being a disciple of Christ.

The Meaning of the Verb "Hate"

What does Jesus mean when He calls his disciples to "hate" father, mother, wife, children, brothers, sisters, and their own lives? The verb "hate" probably reflects a Semitic origin. The Semitic languages often used contrasts to express things in a comparative degree of preferences.[45] Therefore, "to hate" used in this Semitic sense would mean "to love less." I. Howard Marshall affirms such an understanding of the Semitic sense: "this is no doubt how the phrase was understood by Matthew's tradition."[46] It would seem odd for Jesus to instruct His disciples to love their enemies (Luke 6:35) but to hate their families. But when one understands the verb "to hate" in this Semitic sense, one understands that Jesus is calling His disciples to show preference for one over another. David Garland explains that the passage should not be viewed as "I love A and hate B" but should be read "I prefer A to B" ("A" being Jesus and "B" being the list of individuals).[47] The thought then behind the meaning of "hate" is not psychological hate but rather renunciation: "I choose one over another."[48]

The image that is conveyed by this verb is strong. It does not involve a call to be insensitive or to leave all feelings towards our families behind. But following Jesus is to be the disciple's "first love" (Rev 2:4). Being a disciple of Christ should have priority over any family member and even over one's own life. Jesus, and being His disciple, should be the passion of our lives.[49] The idea of "hating" is tantamount to "leaving."[50] To become true disciples of Jesus, the crowds who were following Jesus needed to be willing to part with those individuals closest to their hearts. François Bovon explains the choice that is involved in "hating": "in this connection hate is not, in the first instance, an emotion; it is an act."[51]

With a proper understanding of the verb "hate" in mind, the requirement for discipleship becomes clear. Discipleship to Christ is fundamentally a call to allegiance; as it pertains to importance in a believer's life, Jesus must be first, even above family.[52] One must understand the context of the passage's first-century setting. When a Jewish person made a choice to follow Jesus, he would inevitably alienate his or her family. Darrell Bock explains the cost of discipleship and the level of allegiance required to follow Jesus in a first-century context.

> If someone desired acceptance by family more than
> a relationship with God, one might never come to
> Jesus, given the rejection that would inevitably follow.
> In other words, there could be no casual devotion to

Jesus in the first century. A decision for Christ marked a person and automatically came with a cost.[53]

The language of the passage is clear: if one does not make Jesus the priority of one's life, he/she cannot be His disciple.

If one does not fully forsake his family, he/she will not be fully committed to Christ. Disciples are to distance themselves from the high cultural value placed on family.[54] If a disciple is not diligent, family ties will become a greater pull for one's allegiance than that of Jesus Christ.[55] One's family is not to be the primary priority of one's life; only Jesus is to have that role. David Garland states, "Love for him is to take precedence over all other loves."[56] A disciple must make a choice. He/she cannot have divided loyalties that pull in opposite directions. He/she must be singular in his or her devotion to Jesus Christ.[57]

The Call to Endure Persecution for Christ

In addition to the call for a singular allegiance to Christ, Jesus provides a second requirement to be His disciple. He calls disciples to be willing to endure persecution. In Luke 14:37, Jesus states: "Whoever does not carry his own cross and come after Me cannot be My disciple."

Again, it is of great importance that one understands the first-century context in which this call is found. The call to bear one's cross denotes a willingness to bear the pain of persecution because of following Jesus. It is a call to have a constant willingness to suffer shame and reproach.[58] It is often impossible for 21st-century individuals to understand the shame associated with crucifixion in the ancient world.[59] Crucifixion, understood to be of Persian origin, was a well-known Roman practice during the time of Christ. Crucifixions were such a feared means of execution that various revolts had been suppressed by means of such killings.[60] The horror of this punishment was well known.[61]

35

Jesus calls his disciples to be willing to bear their cross. To "bear one's cross" is not necessarily a call to death. Rather, the call is to the denial of oneself with a willingness to endure hardship which may result in death. To Jesus' Jewish audience, this demand "to bear one's cross" would be understood as an utterly offensive affair. The cross was viewed as "obscene" in the original sense of the word.[62] The illustration is that the disciples must be willing to suffer opposition for Jesus Christ. This opposition may result in death for Christ (martyrdom). A true disciple must be willing to sacrifice all to follow Jesus Christ.

Application for Today

In American churches, persecution and suffering are often viewed as something that should be avoided at all costs. Sadly, most believers will only follow Christ as long as it doesn't cost them too much. Many will only attend church services if they don't conflict with vacations, family plans, activities, sporting events, etc. They will only get involved if the ministry opportunity does not take up too much of their time or energy. Many want to obey God on their terms. They will serve only if it is within their comfort zone and fits into their timeframe. This mindset was exactly what Jesus was addressing in Luke 14. True disciples of Christ must be willing to forsake all to follow Him. Disciples must be singular in their allegiance to Jesus and make Him first place in every area of their lives.

Chapter 4
Principles of Biblical Discipleship, Part II

A S WE OBSERVED IN the last chapter, we are commanded to make disciples (Matt 28:19-20), we are to resemble the Master in all areas of life (Luke 6:40, and we are to be singular in our allegiance to Christ no matter the cost (Luke 14:26-27). In this chapter, we will examine three additional passages which challenge us as disciples and believers in Christ.

John 15:7–8
We Are to Display Specific Characteristics as Disciples of Christ

If you abide in Me, and My words abide in you, ask whatever you wish, and it will be done for you. My Father is glorified by this, that you bear much fruit, and so prove to be My disciples.

In the Upper Room Discourse, Jesus provides four characteristics that should be displayed in the lives of His disciples.

Characteristic 1: Disciples Have an Intimate Relationship with Jesus Christ

The first characteristic of a disciple of Christ is found within the initial phrase: "If you abide in Me." The Greek term for "abide" means "to remain," "to stay," "to wait," "to abide."[1] Gerhard Kittel, in the *Theological Dictionary of the New Testament*, states, "The concept of remaining or abiding takes different forms according to the different relations or antonyms in view."[2] Therefore, the context is the determining factor as to the translation of the term.

In Johannine theology, "abiding" describes the close communion of a believer with Christ.[3] The vine metaphor (John 15:1–6—the preceding context and the continuation of the vine theme into verse 7) illustrates the intimate relationship that Jesus desires with His disciples.[4] Jesus demands that the foundational commitment in a disciple's life is to abide in Him. This means that an intimate relationship with Christ is essential for a disciple. A disciple must be so intimately connected with the Savior that he/she is characterized by the words and actions of Jesus.[5]

Characteristic 2: Disciples have a Passion for the Word of God

Not only does Jesus state that disciples should "abide in Me," but He also expects that "My words abide in you." Just as the disciples were to have an intimate relationship with Christ, God's Word should have an intimate relationship with the disciples. This concept is described by commentators as a "mutual indwelling."[6]

The mutual indwelling described in this passage involves more than just obedience. The idea also entails a continued immersion of Jesus' teaching in one's understanding and life practice.[7] This mutual indwelling is equivalent to doing all that Jesus commands. Don Carson states, "Jesus' words must so lodge in the disciple's mind and heart that conformity to Christ, obedience to Christ, is the most natural (supernatural?) thing in the world."[8] To truly abide in Christ is to allow His words to truly abide within the disciple's life.[9] God's Word continually cleanses the life of a disciple (Ps 119) and therefore must be allowed to "remain" in his daily walk.[10]

> *A disciple's life is marked by Christ, Scripture, prayer, and service.*

Characteristic 3: Disciples have a Consistent Prayer Life

Once disciples display an intimate relationship with Christ and allow God's Word to permeate their lives, they will not only display a dependence on God through prayer, but they will also pray according to God's will. Disciples understand the importance that prayer plays in the life of a believer.[11] This consistent prayer life is displayed in the life of an individual who knows God and seeks to "abide in Him." Jesus assumes ("ask whatever you wish, and it will be done for you") that those who know Him well will ask Him to help in life's situations (cf. Mark 4:35–41).

Leon Morris expounds on the connection of the term "abide" with the answering of the prayers of Jesus' disciples: "When believers abide in Christ and Christ's words abide in them, they live as close to Christ as well may be. Then their prayers will be prayers that are in accord with God's will, and they will be fully answered."[12] A true disciple of Christ proves effective in prayer because what he or she asks for conforms to the will of God.[13]

Characteristic 4: Disciples have a Heart for Ministry and Service

In addition to abiding in Christ, allowing God's Word to remain in them, and having a passion for prayer, disciples desire to serve their Master. "My Father is glorified by this, that you bear much fruit" (John 15:8). The disciples will glorify the Father by their continual fruit-bearing. However, disciples cannot bear fruit of themselves; fruitfulness is confirmation of the God's work in them. The bearing of fruit reveals that they are disciples.[14]

John obviously is writing figuratively when he states that believers should bear much fruit. John is describing the "fruit" of Christian ministry.[15] By involving themselves in Christian service, the disciples will glorify God the Father and prove that they are true disciples.

Application for Today

There are several characteristics that should be evident in the lives of believers found within the pages of Scripture. In John 15:7–8, Jesus provides four main characteristics of His disciples. Disciples are characterized by an intimate relationship with Jesus Christ, a passion for the Bible, a consistent prayer life, and a heart for ministry and service. As described in chapter 1 of this book, recent studies reveal that these characteristics are becoming increasingly rare in the lives of believers. We need to get back to the detailed study of God's Word in the church and in our personal lives. We must have a consistent and meaningful prayer life. We need to have a passion for serving our God—not a service out of duty or obligation, but rather out of a love for our God.

Romans 12:1–2
We Are to Display a Proper Mindset in Relationship to This World

Therefore, I urge you, brethren, by the mercies of God, to present your bodies a living and holy sacrifice, acceptable to God, which is your spiritual service of worship. And do not be conformed to this world, but be transformed by the renewing of your mind, so that you may prove what the will of God is, that which is good and acceptable and perfect.

Though the term "disciple" is not found within Romans 12:1–2, Paul's appeal to the believers in Rome speaks to the mindset that all disciples should exhibit in their spiritual lives. "Therefore" (the first word in English translations but the second word in Greek) demonstrates that Paul wants to show that the teachings of Romans 12:1–15:13 are built firmly on the theology of chapters 1–11. The exhortations and application sections that conclude Romans are firmly built upon the soteriology and sanctification described in Romans 1–11.[16]

The first word of Romans 12:1 carries the plea upon which verses 1 and 2 will be built. The verb for "I urge" has a wide range of meanings including "to call to one's side," "to exhort," "to implore," "to encourage."[17] C. E. B. Cranfield states that the verb is a technical term for Christian exhortation. It is "the earnest appeal, based on the gospel, to those who are already believers to live consistently with the gospel they have received."[18] Robert Mounce reveals the importance of Paul's appeal considering the content that will follow in verses 1–2: "Holiness of life rarely progresses apart from deliberative acts of the will. While sanctification is gradual in the sense that it continues throughout life, each advance depends upon a decision of the will."[19] What has Paul exhorted believers to do?

Believers Are Called to be a Living Sacrifice

In the Septuagint (Greek translation of the Old Testament), "to present" was often used as a technical term for a priest's placing an offering on the altar.[20] In the ancient world the term was also used to describe the presentation of sacrifices.[21] The idea of the term was to indicate a "surrendering" for sacrifice or "yielding up" for the altar.[22] However, sacrifices of dead animals on an altar (as practiced in the Old Testament) are no longer acceptable to God. Jesus Christ, being the perfect Lamb of God (John 1:29), was sacrificed once for all in our place.[23] Christians are not to offer animals to God but rather to offer themselves to God as "living sacrifices."[24]

Paul's use of sacrificial imagery here is a pattern that is used throughout the New Testament. As stated above, Christians no longer offer literal sacrifices to Christ because He has fulfilled, through His death, the requirements for salvation ending the Old Testament sacrificial system. However, with the common understanding of sacrifice in ancient religious systems, using sacrificial imagery was an important tool to convey the spiritual convictions of the early church.[25]

That the sacrifice is "living" reflects the voluntary nature of the act. F. F. Bruce comments that "the sacrifices of the new order do not consist in taking the lives of others, like the ancient animal sacrifices, but in giving one's own (Heb 13:15–16; 1 Pet 2:5)."[26] Paul qualifies the sacrifice that we offer by stating that it is a "living" sacrifice. This adjective refers "to the nature of the sacrifice itself: one that does not die as it is offered but goes on living and therefore continues in its efficacy until the person who is offered dies."[27] John MacArthur explains that the "living" sacrifice we are to offer "is the willingness to surrender to Him all our hopes, plans, and everything that is precious to us, all that is humanly important to us, all that we find fulfilling."[28] Believers are called upon to make an ongoing sacrifice of not only their lives but also their desires.

When Paul calls believers to offer their "bodies" as living sacrifices, the term "bodies" is to be interpreted as the entirety of the individual.[29] Wright describes it as "the complete person seen from one point of view: the point of view in which the human being lives as a physical object within space and time."[30] The sacrifice that Paul exhorts believers to offer is their "bodies" themselves. Unlike the Old Testament sacrificial system in which the gift was of central importance (Gen 4:3–7),[31] God, in the New Testament sacrificial imagery, demands the giver himself.[32] This reemphasizes once again the aspect of "living" sacrifice. Colin Kruse states, "Paul employs the idea of a 'living sacrifice' deliberately because the sacrifice he has in mind is not martyrdom, but rather lives that are pleasing to God."[33] Paul is making a special point to emphasize that this sacrifice is not once and done. Instead, the sacrifice calls for continual dedication to the service of God even in the face of opposition from the world.[34]

This type of ongoing, living, dedicated sacrifice of our bodies is "holy and pleasing to God." Believers must realize that the possibility of bringing pleasure to God should provide a powerful motivation for the complete surrender of our will and self to Him.[35] "Holy" is a regular description of sacrifices in the Old Testament (cf. Num 18). The idea behind the term implies that the offering is "set apart" from the profane and is dedicated to God. Likewise, as "living" sacrifices believers are to be "set apart" from this world.[36]

Paul said that the offering of one's body as a "living sacrifice" is a "spiritual act of worship." It is the reasonable act of service (worship) by Christians. God is not asking disciples to do something that is impossible or unthinkable. Instead, dedicating one's life to serving God should be a reasonable sacrifice by those who have been redeemed by the death of Christ.[37]

Believers Are Commanded Not to Conform to the World's System

After Paul's exhortation to "present your bodies as living sacrifices," he urges Christians to involve themselves in two ongoing activities. These activities reveal how the believer is to become an acceptable "living sacrifice." The first activity is negative in nature; the second activity is positive. First, believers are no longer to "conform themselves" to the world's system.[38] The term for "conform" means to "squeeze you into its own mold."[39]

Paul's command that we "not be conformed to this world" calls Christians to resist the pressure to "be squeezed into the mold" of this world. Believers are not to fall into the "pattern" of behavior that typifies the world's system.[40] Disciples are to think differently than the world's mindset. Disciples should have a different perspective on life, and their actions should demonstrate this alternate viewpoint. This leads to the second, positive, activity.

Believers Are Commanded to Be Transformed by the Renewing of Their Mind

Instead of being fitted into the world's mold, believers are commanded to be "transformed by the renewing of your mind." The verb is present tense and therefore describes a continuing process of constant transformation.[41] This transformation is not a once and done activity but rather a consistent work of being altered in one's thinking. The verb occurs in two other settings in the New Testament. In Mark 9:2 (Matt 17:2) Jesus "transfigured" before His three disciples. In 2 Corinthians 3:18,

Paul taught that believers who behold the glory of the Lord are being "transformed" into His likeness. The transformation Paul is describing in Romans 12:2 is not a change effected from outside the individual but rather a radical reorientation that begins deep within the human heart.[42]

"The renewing of your mind" is how this transformation takes place. "Mind" is a word that Paul uses specifically to indicate a person's "practical reason" or "moral consciousness."[43] In other words, Christians are to adjust their way of thinking. This process does not occur overnight but is a lifelong process of altering one's thinking to resemble the way that God desires that a person think about life and service.[44]

There is continuing pressure by the "world" on disciples to adopt the customs and mind-set of the world in which they live. Though Christians may reject that pressure, this action alone will never create the kind of change God has in mind for his followers. Real and lasting change comes from within.[45] Disciples must let themselves be transformed by the "renewing of the mind." How this process is accomplished will be addressed in chapter seven. A renewed mind is concerned with those issues of life that are of lasting importance.[46]

> *A disciple must rethink & reform his relationship to the world.*

Application for Today

Many believers do not view their lives as a form of sacrifice for their Savior. Instead, believers live their lives for their own comforts, wants, and needs. Paul exhorts us to view life as a "living sacrifice." For most, life is about them. As disciples of Jesus our mindset should be about putting Christ first in all areas of our lives. Our desire should be to please Him before pleasing self. Our lives should be a living sacrifice to Him. To clarify, this sacrifice should be "holy" unto God. Are we remaining pure in our daily walk with God? Or are we being "pressed into the mold" of the world (its passions, desires, temptations, mind-set)?

2 Timothy 2:2
We Are to Replicate Ourselves
into the Lives of Others

The things which you have heard from me in the presence of many witnesses, entrust these to faithful men who will be able to teach others also.

What has Timothy Learned?

Paul urges Timothy to entrust "things which you heard from me" to faithful men who teach those "things" to others. What is it that Timothy has learned from Paul? What Timothy is to pass along to "faithful men" appears to be mentioned first in 2 Timothy 1:13–14: "Retain the standard of sound words which you have heard from me, in the faith and love which are in Christ Jesus. Guard, through the Holy Spirit who dwells in us, the treasure which has been entrusted to you." The "sound words" mentioned in 1:13 and the "things" mentioned again in 2:2 are the foundational truths of the gospel.[47] The preeminence of the gospel in Paul's preaching is a common thread that is seen throughout Paul's writings. From his first letter on, the gospel has become the central focus of his preaching.[48] Timothy is to entrust the treasure of gospel truths to others.[49]

Though the gospel is clearly a component of the "things" Paul is describing in 2 Timothy 2:2, Paul appears to have in mind an additional component as well. Dibelius, Conzelmann, Knight, and others suggest that "what you have heard" refers to a formulated summary of his teachings (1 Cor 15:3ff).[50] Paul wants Timothy to entrust to others the "traditions" that he has received from Paul (cf. 2 Thess 2:15).[51] Timothy has received teaching from Paul over a period of several years. Through his extensive travel with Paul and his ministry alongside of Paul at Ephesus, Timothy has been taught foundational truths.[52]

What Is Timothy to Do with the Learning?

Timothy is commanded to take "the things" (that which has been deposited to him by Paul) and entrust them to faithful men who will then teach "the things" to others. The chain of teaching, the "tradition," is therefore continued generation to generation.[53] This passage reveals that Paul was concerned that the foundational truths of the gospel were both guarded and accurately transmitted from one generation of Christians to another (2 Tim 1:13–14).[54]

William Barclay states, "The teacher is a link in the living chain which stretches unbroken from this present moment back to Jesus Christ. The glory of teaching is that it links the present with the earthly life of Jesus Christ."[55] The first stage in the spiritual "relay" was "these things" being handed from Paul to Timothy. Timothy's obligation was to "run the second lap" in which he was to entrust the things he had been taught by Paul to faithful men.[56] "Entrusting" these foundational truths of the gospel was not simply tapping another believer on the shoulder and providing basic encouragement. Rather, it would require Timothy to teach and to model the faith before people who in turn would teach and model it before others.[57]

For this teaching to pass from generation to generation, it is essential that people of character continue to teach the true gospel. It is imperative that Timothy identify these men and entrust the gospel to them before he departs. By identifying "faithful men," he will ensure the integrity of the gospel message as it is passed on.[58] Another quality of these individuals who are to pass on these foundational truths is that they have the ability to teach others.[59] They had to be "qualified to teach others." They had to "be able and competent in turn to pass on to others this treasure by their ability and willingness to teach."[60] Paul is urging Timothy to entrust the foundational truths of the gospel in a systematic way to faithful people who can teach others.

The Pattern of Replication

Second Timothy 2:2 provides the pattern of replication in discipleship: entrust the foundational truths of the gospel to faithful people, who in turn will entrust the truths to other faithful people. This pattern of replication is expressed clearly in the book of Acts. In Acts 9 and 11, Barnabas encouraged a new believer, Paul, introducing him to believers at Jerusalem who were reticent to get close to Paul because of his former reputation. Barnabas had a discipling/mentoring relationship with Paul. Later in the book of Acts, as an established believer, Paul entrusted to young believers, Aquila and Priscilla, the truths of Scripture (Acts 18). Aquila and Priscilla, after maturing in their faith, taught the truths they learned from Paul to Apollos (Acts 18:24–26). This pattern, which is explained in 2 Timothy 2:2 and revealed in Acts, provides the ongoing pattern of discipleship: the church is to train young believers to maturity, who will then continue to teach and train other young believers.

Application for Today

Expounding upon the command of Matthew 28:19–20, Paul challenges us to reproduce ourselves spiritually in the lives of others. We stand as a link in a long chain connected back to the apostles. We are to take the biblical teaching that has been entrusted in us by others and pass that biblical teaching on to others. Are you faithfully reproducing yourself spiritually in the lives of others? Are we teaching the truths of Scripture to our children, new believers, younger men, younger women, etc.? The link in the chain can be broken if one generation does not teach the next generation.

Summary Chart of Principles of Biblical Discipleship

Make disciples—Matt 28:19–20
> Imperative nature of the command
> How to disciple: Baptism & teaching

Resemble the Master in all areas of life—Luke 6:40
> Nature of instruction: Reordering one's life
> Content of instrution: Experience and character
> Goal of instruction: Become like Him

Be singular in allegiance to Christ—Luke 14:26–27
> No matter the cost, even hatred
> Willingness to endure persecution

Specific characteristics of life—John 15:7–8
> Intimate relationship with Jesus
> Passion for the Word of God
> Consistent prayer life
> A heart for ministry and service

Proper mindset in relation to the world—Rom 12:1–2
> A living sacrifice
> Not conforming to the world
> Transformed by the renewing of mind

Replicate in the lives of others—2 Tim 2:2
> Recognizing what is learned
> Entrusting others with what is learned

Chapter 5
Key Factors in Discipleship Today

CONSIDERING THE CURRENT TRENDS that we are facing in the church and in Christianity today, it is critical that we return to biblical discipleship in the church, in our homes, and in our individual spiritual lives. This chapter will examine how biblical discipleship requires an understanding of three key factors: the role of God's Word, the role of church and believer, and the role of teachers and mentors.

Before we dive into how to disciple today, it is important that we address a major issue: the lack of actual teaching and preaching of God's Word. Sadly, the Bible has taken a backseat to stories, illustrations, humor, etc. in our teaching. As an individual who has a doctorate in education, I understand better than most the importance of proper communication skills and techniques, learning theory, active learning, differentiated instruction, etc. However, churches today are minimizing the expositional preaching and teaching of God's Word. Most of our worship time is spent singing instead of preaching. Our Sunday School time is spent taking prayer requests and updating each other about our lives instead of teaching the Scriptures.

Singing, praying, and fellowship are critical in the spiritual life of individuals and the church; however, we are giving most of our time together to these activities and minimal time to the study of God's Word.

I have observed that in small group studies much of the time is filled with informing the group about the details of one's week and updates on family dynamics and a small amount of time in biblical study. Again, these issues are important for fellowship, but the main component of discipleship is growth in and through God's Word. We would do well to return to indepth Bible study. To grow deeper spiritually, we must spend time in God's Word mining the rich truths contained within the Bible. We must return to the Book. It is critically important that we understand the importance of God's Word in the discipleship process. It is through the study of the Bible that people grow and are changed spiritually.

Factor 1
The Importance of God's Word in Discipleship

All Scripture is inspired by God and profitable for teaching, for reproof, for correction, for training in righteousness; so that the man of God may be adequate, equipped for every good work. (2 Tim 3:16–17)

One of the most significant passages of Scripture describing the importance of God's Word is 2 Timothy 3:16–17. Paul instructs Timothy that all of Scripture comes from God and is critical to the growth of believers. It is the Word that transforms a life. It is the Word that develops individuals into disciples of Christ.

Paul states that all Scripture comes from God. There is some debate over this concept. Lea and Griffin in their commentary on this passage accurately state the following:

> It is clear from the context that Paul was not merely referring to a single passage of Scripture. He was making either a collective reference to all of Scripture or a partitive reference to each passage of Scripture.... If we affirm that each part of Scripture is inspired, we come eventually to assert that its entire content is inspired.[1]

Some argue that the term *all* should be translated *every*. The result of this translation (*every*) can suggest that only some portions of Scripture are inspired. This is a foreign concept for Paul in writing to Timothy. Paul rather argues that every portion of Scripture is inspired and forms a cohesive whole. The entirety of Scripture comes from God Himself.[2]

Knight highlights that whether we use the term *all* or *every*, the result is still the same: God is the author of the whole of Scripture. "In the final analysis there is no essential difference in meaning. 'All scripture' perceives scripture as a whole, and 'every scripture' perceives it in terms of all its component parts."[3]

Not only is every word and all of Scripture from God, it is also inspired or "breathed out" from Him. The Greek word for inspired is the combination of two Greek words: *theos* meaning "God" and *pneustos* meaning "breathed."[4] When taken together, the Greek word for *inspired* means to be "breathed out of God." It is literally from God Himself. He is the source of Scripture. It is His literal words to us. Lea and Griffin highlight the importance of the Greek term:

The idea the term presents is that God has breathed his character into Scripture so that it is inherently inspired. Paul was not asserting that the Scriptures are inspiring in that they breathe information about God into us, even though the statement is true. The Scriptures owe their origin and distinctiveness to God himself. This is the abiding character of Scripture.[5]

When we contemplate the idea of "God breathed," we are reminded of when God breathed into Adam and gave him life. The concept of "God breathed" can be seen in Genesis 2:7 where Moses writes: "Then the LORD God formed man of dust from the ground, and breathed into his nostrils the breath of life; and man became a living being." Similarly, God has breathed out the Bible, and it is the life source for believers.

How Is the Bible Beneficial to My Life?

Second Timothy 3:16–17 addresses the benefits that Scripture has in the life of a believer. These benefits are timeless in their application to lives. Paul states that the Bible is *profitable.* The meaning of the Greek word informs us that the Bible is useful, beneficial to equip the believer for life.[6]

From what we have observed from this text, the Bible is the basis for all truth and is essential for our spiritual life. The Scriptures bring great benefit to the life of the believer! In what ways is Scripture beneficial to our lives?

- *Doctrine*—teachings of Scripture, instruction in the truths of God's Word. Doctrine shows you the path God has designed.

- *Reproof*—convincing one of his/her sin; it also carries the idea of rebuking, pointing out the sin in one's life. Reproof points out when you stepped off the path.

- *Correction*—correcting faults, setting to right, restoration. Correction shows you how to get back onto the path.

- *Training in righteousness*—moral training that leads us to living righteously before God. Training in righteousness keeps us on the right path.

Analogy of the Pathway

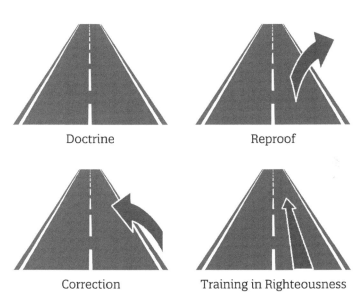

Doctrine   Reproof

Correction   Training in Righteousness

The Bible is beneficial to you and me because it reveals to us what God desires from us. It points out when we have sinned and disobeyed God. It shows us how to repent and realign our desires with God's plan. It discloses how to continually walk according to God's commands.

What Will Happen as I Study Scripture?

The two Greek words that are used in 2 Timothy 3:17 to describe how we are prepared for good works are very descriptive in their meanings. The first term means to be "in fit shape or condition."[7] The second term means to be "equipped, prepared, or qualified."[8] The Greek terms reveal that the Christian who studies God's Word will be in shape and ready/prepared completely to do whatever God calls them to do. It reveals that studying Scripture prepares you for the future things God calls and leads you to do.[9] Each Christian will be thoroughly prepared to live according to godly behavior. In addition, he/she will be prepared to minister to others and serve God as well.[10] Next, the church can—and should—provide structure and opportunities for discipleship of believers.

Factor 2
Correcting Misunderstandings about Discipleship

Sadly, in American churches today, many people simply come to church to be a number, an unrecognizable name, a person in the pew that slips out after the service; they fail to make a lasting impact on other members of the church. They are more comfortable this way since they can remain anonymous and "check the box" as a Christian. Oftentimes, these individuals believe that a one-hour dose of church on Sunday is all they really need to grow. With this low level of commitment and exposure to God's Word, their lives may be impacted slightly, but it is not the characteristic of a true disciple of Christ or a mature believer.

My pastor, Stephen Davey, shared an illustration of this mindset with the church's new members class. He asked, "If you were allowed to only eat one meal a week, how healthy would you be?" During that meal you could eat anything that you wanted and whatever quantity that you wanted. You could have chicken, steak, vegetables, starches, desserts, etc. Whatever your heart's desire is; you could eat that food. However, that's the only meal you could eat for the whole week. How would you feel after four days or after six days? You would be anemic. You would feel terrible. You would be extremely hungry. You would be malnourished and unhealthy. Sadly, that is what many Christians allow themselves to experience on a regular basis. They are only exposed to the meat of God's Word for one hour each week. That little exposure to God's Word will leave a Christian anemic. A healthy believer must be in God's Word far more than simply one hour per week.

It is imperative that the church provide discipleship opportunities for the growth of its members. Even though not all individuals will attend each of these ministries, the opportunities for spiritual growth must be provided by the church. In addition, people need to be challenged to become more engaged and involved within the body of Christ (1 Cor 12:12–31). Each member of the body is a critical component to the health and strength of the body as a whole. Without healthy members, the body suffers. Without mature believers, the church suffers as well.

Now it is important to note that the available ministries that a church can offer its members vary depending on size, location, personality, available staff, etc. However, I would argue that a church should provide as many of these opportunities as it can since this will only strengthen the growth and maturity of its members.

How do we get people more involved in the discipleship process? How do we push against the growing trend of inactivity among church goers? Churches must be intentional about the teaching and preaching of God's Word! Churches must be intentional in their discipleship process.

Historically, being a Christian described one's life (Acts 11:26). Followers of Jesus were first called "Christians" in the city of Antioch. Acts 11:26 says, "For an entire year they [Paul and Barnabas] met with the church and taught considerable numbers; and the disciples were first called Christians in Antioch." They were called "Christians" because their speech, behavior, and lifestyle were like Christ.

John Polhill, in his commentary on Acts, describes the significance of this term "Christian."

> The term "Christian" was first applied to disciples in Antioch. This may be of more significance than might appear on first sight. The term only occurs in two other places in the New Testament (Acts 26:28; 1 Pet 4:16). In all three instances it is a term used by outsiders to designate Christians. Evidently the term was not originally used by Christians of themselves. They preferred terms like "believers, disciples, brothers."[11]

In addition, F. F. Bruce describes the lifestyle that these early believers exemplified toward the outside world.

> The church of Antioch from the outset had an *ethos* quite distinct from that of the Jerusalem church. The pagans of Antioch, too, knew all about these people, for they did not keep quiet about their faith, but proclaimed it wherever they went.... "Who are these people?" one Antiochene would ask another, as two or three unofficial missionaries gathered a knot of more or less interested hearers and disputants around them in one of the city colonnades. "Oh, these are the people who are always talking about *Christos*, the Christ-people, the Christians." Just as, in Pales-

tine, the adherents of the Herod dynasty were called Herodians, so, says Luke, in Antioch the adherents of Jesus the Christ first came to be popularly known as Christians.[12]

The Christian life was not simply a Sunday phenomenon to the early church. Christianity was not something that they simply practiced one day a week. Christianity—being a Christ follower (a disciple of Jesus)—was their life.

Sadly, many believers today do not live their lives as if Christianity is their lifestyle. I have often commented in my classes that most believers live their lives as if they were "practical atheists." What do I mean by that phrase? Most Christians go through their lives without reading God's Word on a regular basis and without a consistent prayer life. They will go through their day without consulting God, without talking to others about Him, without turning to Him with their concerns or asking Him for help with their life situations. They go through life as if they do not even need God. They are living like "practical atheists." This should not be the case in the life of a disciple of Christ. As Christians (little Christs, or Christ followers), our lives should be distinctive. People should know that we are different than those who do not know the Savior. Teachers and mentors play an important part in establishing this mindset.

Factor 3
The Role of Teachers and Mentors in Discipleship

Ephesians 4:11–16 is an important passage regarding the role that gifted individuals (apostles, prophets, evangelists, pastors, and teachers) have in the growth and maturity of disciples of Christ. Within this group, there is a specific group labeled pastors and teachers. The role of both pastor and teacher was to teach the Word of God to the believers within the churches. With regular corporate instruction by both pastors and teachers, believers were challenged to grow spiritually. Pastors and teachers did not simply convey information, they urged the hearers to live by what they had been taught (Eph. 4:20–21).[13] What are the primary functions of the pastors and teachers for the church?

Equipping the Saints to do the Work of the Ministry

"Equipping" refers to that which is "fit, is restored to its original condition, or is made complete." The word was used in nautical settings to describe "refitting a ship" or in medical situations for the "setting of bones."[14] The term indicates in Ephesians 4:12 that the "gifts" are provided to "fit out" saints to do God's service. Paul's language, "for the equipping of the saints for the work of service," indicates that it is not the "gifted individuals" who are to do all the work of service.[15] Obviously, the "gifted individuals" share in doing the work of the ministry, but God's basic design is for the saints to be equipped so that they can serve each other effectively.[16] Clinton Arnold clarifies that "Christ has given gifted leaders to the church not merely to do the ministry, but to invest their time heavily in developing and preparing fellow believers to engage in ministry to the body."[17] The model Paul is proposing to the church is of mutual service and not of professionals serving a group of consumers.[18]

In conclusion, Christ gave "gifts" (pastors, elders and deacons, teachers, etc.) to the church for the immediate purpose of preparing all the saints for service to build up the entire body of Christ. As each believer carries out his/her work, the church will be built up. The idea that ministry belongs to the clergy and not to the saints is foreign to this context because every saint is involved in the ministry.[19]

Leading the Saints to Maturity
in Their Spiritual Walks

Once Paul establishes that the gifted people were given to the church for the immediate purpose of preparing all the saints to minister for the building up of the body of Christ, he explains the need for the process for believers to mature to the measure of the fullness of Christ. The adjective that is used means "having reached its end, complete, or accomplished."[20] The term is used of sacrifices that are "perfect, without spot/blemish," of animals that are "fully grown," and of a person who is "fully grown" or "matured" as opposed to an infant or child.[21]

In contrast to the mature believers, the immature believers are described as "infants or very young children."[22] The term suggests not only physical age but childish understanding, foolishness, inexperience, or lack of insight.[23] New Testament writers use the term "infants" to represent spiritual immaturity.[24] The nature of the children's immaturity is graphically pictured in Ephesians 4:14. These infants are unstable, lacking in direction, vacillating, and open to manipulation. Like a small, rudderless boat, they are tossed back and forth by the waves. They are continually driven back and forth by the different winds of teaching.

It is important to examine the participles that describe the infants. "Being tossed back and forth by the waves and carried about by every wind of doctrine"—describes one who is childish and lacks stability. The first participle implies that the person is thrown around by the waves of the sea and cast into confusion. The meaning of Ephesians 4:14 reflects that this spiritually immature believer is easily confused in their thinking and easily influenced by other teachers.[25] The second participle, "turn around or make dizzy," indicates a level of confusion by the spiritually immature believer. Both participles are passive, indicating that an outside force—"false teachers" or "false teaching"—is causing the confusion.[26]

"Every wind of doctrine" indicates false teaching that stands against the unity of faith and knowledge contained within the Scriptures (v. 13). Paul's reference is best understood as the various religious philosophies and systems which threatened to undermine or dilute the gospel message.[27] The teaching that is causing the confusion is false teaching designed to counteract that of the pastors and teachers (v. 11).[28] The pastors and teachers bring stability and unity, whereas false teachings bring confusion, turmoil, and disunity. The false teaching is meant to confuse and swirl one around violently, causing dizziness.[29]

Paul provides this important text for the church to reveal the "gifts" (gifted individuals) that God has given to the saints to enable them to serve Him. God provided these gifted individuals to the church to equip the saints to do His work, to bring unity to the body, to bring believers from infancy to maturity, and to establish believers so that they are not tossed about by false teaching. True disciples of Christ reveal that they are established and grounded in God's Word and are actively participating in the work of the ministry.

Chapter 6
Discipleship Avenues for the Church

THERE IS OFTEN MISUNDERSTANDING as to what discipleship is and how it should be accomplished in the church. Part of the reason for this misunderstanding is that individuals have defined aspects of discipleship as discipleship itself. For instance, I've heard it said, "If a church does not have small groups, then they are not doing discipleship." Small groups are a critical component of discipleship. However, they are just one aspect of discipleship, not discipleship entirely.

It is important to remember the definition of discipleship. Discipleship is *the process of learning the teachings of Scripture, internalizing them to shape one's belief system, and then acting upon them in one's daily life.* That process is done in a variety of ways and in a variety of settings in the church.

It is important to view discipleship as an umbrella. Under that umbrella are many "ribs" or supports that strengthen the umbrella. Several of those ribs in a church setting are preaching, Sunday school, adult Bible fellowships, small groups, missional teams, mentoring, and coaching. A healthy church will incorporate a number of those ribs so that the discipleship process impacts numerous members and congregants in the church.

The following are several key avenues or "ribs" under the umbrella of discipleship that are critical to the growth of an individual spiritually. Members of the church need to be challenged to become involved in these aspects or "ribs" of the ministry. As they attend, receive instruction and teaching, and serve in these ministries, they grow as disciples of Christ.

I believe that four key areas of ministry must each become part of a believer's/disciple's life. It is important that you understand two main implications from this perspective.

- We must *stop* expecting complete discipleship to take place in just one or two of the avenues of ministry.

- We must *start* a sustainable pattern of discipleship that incorporates these four areas of ministry for believers to be discipled in the church.[1]

The four main teaching avenues for the church to help disciples grow spiritually are 1) The Preaching Ministry, 2) The Teaching Ministry, 3) The Small Group Ministry, and 4) The Mentoring Ministry.

As we examine these four areas of discipleship ministry that should be found in our churches, it is important to begin by looking at Jesus' ministry, then to examine the responsibility and roles of the teacher in each ministry setting. Lastly, we'll examine the discipleship aim in each ministry setting.

The Preaching Ministry (Worship Service)

The preaching ministry, as an avenue of discipleship, serves to challenge individuals in their personal walk with the Lord through the public proclamation of the Word of God. The aim is to leave disciples challenged, encouraged, and equipped spiritually to serve the Lord in their daily lives.

Jesus and the Crowds

Throughout Jesus' ministry, we see Him interacting with and teaching large crowds. Because of His ability to perform miracles and His masterful teaching, Jesus drew large crowds to Himself. In Matthew 5–7, we read the longest sermon recorded by Jesus (The Sermon on the Mount). In Matthew 5:1-2 Matthew writes, "When Jesus saw the crowds, He went up on the mountain; and after He sat down, His disciples came to Him. And He opened His mouth and *began* to teach them." There are a couple of important points to notice here.

Preaching should challenge, encourage, and equip disciples.

First, Jesus was teaching a large crowd. Though the size of the crowd is not recorded, it is a larger gathering involving both the inner circle of disciples and a larger gathering of individuals. As Grant Osborne highlights, Jesus had "a desire to address the disciples particularly, involving an inner circle (the disciples, active participants) and an outer circle (the crowds, passive participants)."[2] Second, the entire group of listeners are referred to as disciples. I would agree with Louis Barbieri when he states that "'Disciples' refers not to the Twelve, as some suggest, but to the crowds following Him."[3] There is a discipleship component in the public teaching ministry of Jesus to the crowds that followed Him.

In John 6:1–15 we read of another occasion in Jesus' ministry where He ministered to a significant crowd. In this passage, we read of the incredible miracle of the feeding of the 5,000. This passage reveals to us the sheer size of the crowds that came to listen to Jesus. Edwin Blum describes the crowd: "the people were seated in groups of 50 and 100. This made the crowd easy to count and the food easy to distribute. Five thousand men were there, plus women and children (Matt. 14:21). Thus probably more than 10,000 people were fed."[4]

One of the main discipleship avenues for Jesus was the teaching of the crowds (disciples). Jesus' teaching ministry stands as our chief example of how to address/teach individuals in different group sizes. Jesus was the quintessential teacher. He provided the teaching template. He was the ultimate authority and prototype for teaching. Interestingly, in the Gospels, one of the most frequently used designations for Jesus was "Teacher." He is called "Teacher" forty-five times in the Gospels.[5]

When we examine the methods that Jesus used to teach others, we see a basis for us as ministers to reflect upon as we ourselves teach others. His methods are tried and true. Two thousand years later, modern educational techniques reflect what Jesus practiced as a teacher in His day. Jesus teaching was creative, unique, engaging, and developmental.

First, Jesus' teaching was creative. Jesus would ask probing questions: Do you believe that I am able to do this? (Matt 9:28); Who do people say that I am? (Mark 8:27–30); Which of the two did what his father wanted? (Matt 21:31); Which of these three do you think was a neighbor? (Luke 10:36). In addition, Jesus used parables to teach heavenly truths by using earthly stories (Matt 13:10-11). Thirty-five percent of His recorded teachings were in the form of parables.[6] Also, Jesus employed a number of other creative methods in delivering His message: proverbs (Mark 6:4), paradox (Mark 12:41–44), irony (Matt 16:2–3), hyperbole (Matt 23:23–24), simile (Luke 13:34), puns (Matt 16:18), allusion (John 2:19), and metaphor (Luke 13:32).[7]

Second, Jesus' teaching was unique. As Howard Hendricks observes, each lesson was uniquely crafted to meet the needs of the learner.

Every lesson was hand-tooled and chosen to fit the demands of the situation and the needs of the learner. Every encounter was distinctively different because He knew what was in man generally and individually (John 2:24–25). The three interviews that follow (Nicodemus, the Samaritan woman, and the nobleman of Capernaum), demonstrate His ability to deal skillfully and uniquely with three different types of personalities. The goal was identical—to bring them to faith. The methodology was different.[8]

Jesus understood the needs of each individual and uniquely crafted His teaching lesson to both meet those needs and challenge the individual to faith.

Ronald Allen summarizes the uniqueness of Christ's teaching, which often contradicts the modern understanding of a great teacher.

We tend to link a great teacher with a great institution. Jesus had no such ties. We tend to think of a great teacher as one who makes difficult things less complex. Jesus seemed to show new complexities even in simple things. We tend to anticipate that a great teacher helps us face life more independently. Jesus kept insisting that life must be lived in full dependence on another. We tend to associate a great teacher with technical language of his or her field. Jesus used simple language and everyday things. We tend to link a great teacher to his or her brilliant, erudite students. Those who learned best from Jesus were the poor, the lonely, and the simple. We tend to think of a great teacher in the setting of a classroom. Jesus' classroom was a hillside overlooking the Sea of Galilee, a corner of a living room, a walk along a path, a small space in a little boat. Today we tend to look for a teacher to use multimedia tools. Jesus' tools were the heavens, the fields, mountains and birds, storms and sheep, a vineyard, a well, and a banquet. In short, whatever was around He would use as a teaching tool.[9]

Third, Jesus' teaching was engaging. Throughout Jesus' teaching ministry, a problem-solving mentality was used to draw individuals to become involved in the teaching process. "He engaged people by presenting a problem, by asking an appropriate question, by using repetition, by telling a story or simply by maintaining silence" (Luke 10:25–37).[10]

Lastly, Jesus' teaching was developmental. "Our Lord's goal was to take people from where they were to where they ought to be…. From our Lord we learn that good teaching involves helping the learner to assume responsibility for his thinking and living. He was forever encouraging and enabling people to make the best possible choices."[11]

> *Jesus' teaching was creative, unique, engaging, & developmental.*

The Responsibility and Role of the Preacher

The most relevant demonstration of Jesus' public ministry in our contexts would be the preaching ministry of the church. Through the Sunday morning preaching service, the pastor teaches larger crowds (depending on the size of the church).

It is critical for pastors to understand the importance of their role in the life of a believer. Because this role is so critical to the spiritual growth of fellow Christians, God places an incredible responsibility on those who fill the pastoral role. We need to remember that God holds us accountable. This is not a position to be entered into lightly. James 3:1 warns us of the importance of the pastoral role: "Do not become teachers in large numbers, my brothers, since you know that we *who are teachers* will incur a stricter judgment" (NASB).

In addition, Paul challenges his young disciple in the faith (Timothy) to understand the ministry he is called to fulfill as a pastor. Second Timothy 4:1–5 reads,

> I solemnly exhort you in the presence of God and of Christ Jesus, who is to judge the living and the dead, and by His appearing and His kingdom: preach the word; be ready in season and out of season; correct, rebuke, and exhort, with great patience and instruction. For the time will come when they will not tolerate sound doctrine; but wanting to have their ears tickled, they will accumulate for themselves teachers in accordance with their own desires, and they will turn their ears away from the truth and will turn aside to myths. But as for you, use self-restraint in all things, endure hardship, do the work of an evangelist, fulfill your ministry (NASB).

As one studies this passage, several features appear that remind us of this important calling of the preaching ministry. First, we need to remember the seriousness of this calling. In verse one, Paul states that Jesus is our judge. God Himself watches and observes our preaching ministry. He is the One who will one day evaluate and judge how we preached His Word.

Second, we need to remember the substance of this calling. In verse two, Paul states that we are to "preach the word." Many preachers spend their time telling stories, using humor, and "performing" before their congregations as they "preach" their sermons. It is important to understand and utilize appropriate communication techniques. I teach classes on communication skills and understand the importance of utilizing the best practices for communicating truth. However, many preachers spend more time polishing their sermons than preparing their sermons from the text. We are called to preach the "word." Are we handling Scripture accurately? Are we spending adequate time in exegetical study of the Bible?

Third, we are to remember the timeliness of this calling. Again, Paul states to Timothy in verses 2 and 3 that we need to be ready all the time to "preach the word" because the time is coming when "they will not tolerate sound doctrine." Preachers, we are in that time! This world does not tolerate the truths, principles, and commands of God's Word. The importance of the preacher cannot be minimized! We have a sincere calling to preach God's Word. We must follow Paul's admonition to "correct, rebuke, and exhort, with great patience and instruction."

Discipleship in the Preaching Ministry

Though the preaching ministry may not be the deepest level of discipleship for a believer's life, it is still a critical component in the spiritual growth of individual disciples. Regular exposure to the preaching of God's Word is critical to the diet of disciples. The pastor can share very personal truths but in an impersonal way. What I mean by this is that a pastor may touch on very personal sin issues in the life of a believer and yet not single out that individual. Also, preaching can tackle difficult topics which may produce awkwardness or be viewed as intrusive if spoken about in a smaller setting. Through preaching, the pastor can share vision and central teaching that can reach many individuals at one single time. Lastly, preaching can call for a spiritual response while still allowing for a level of anonymity.[12] Ultimately, spiritual transparency is the goal of the discipleship process, but early in the journey, new believers may struggle with allowing their lives to be seen under the microscope. Preaching allows for the message of God's Word to pierce the heart while allowing individuals to personally examine their lives privately. "Preaching … is an important part of our growth as disciples of Jesus. Through these times we receive teaching that will fuel our discipleship journey as we go back out to our places of mission."[13]

The Teaching Ministry (Sunday School, Adult Bible Fellowships, Teen Classes, Children's Classes, Men's Ministry, Women's Ministry, College, Etc.)

Another critical avenue of discipleship ministry in the church is the teaching ministry. Different than the preaching ministry, the teaching ministry is designed for classes ranging anywhere from 15–100 depending on the size of the church. This specific avenue of discipleship is designed for people to "relate and connect, and discipleship occurs through community, mission, and practice."[14]

Jesus and the Wider Group of Disciples

Jesus' ministry is often divided between His interactions with the crowds that followed Him and His interactions with His twelve disciples. However, there is a middle-sized group of individuals that Jesus spent a vast amount of time with and sent out on mission for Him. In Luke 10:1–20, we are introduced to a unique missional task that Jesus sent this larger group of disciples on to pave the way for His ministry. Jesus sent His disciples out in groups of two to prepare the towns and regions for His arrival. David Garland describes this unique missional approach that Jesus used in Luke 10.

> The pairs provide the double witness prescribed in
> Deut 17:6; 19:15. In addition, going out in pairs pro-

vides companionship, some protection, and accountability. There is no parallel in Jewish history for one to
send out others on a mission to proclaim news about
the reign of God, and the authority for this action is
located in Jesus' own person. This harvest is part of
"the long-promised gathering of the people of God
(Isa 27:12)."[15]

From this text, we see that Jesus used His large group of
disciples as missionaries preparing the way for His arrival and
subsequent teaching.

In Luke 8:1–3, Jesus is described as teaching, preaching,
and bringing the good news of the kingdom of God. Accompa-
nying Him were the Twelve, but also a large group of disciples
including various women who helped support His mission.
This larger group of disciples was taught by Jesus and supported Him on His journeys.

In Luke 6:12–13, Jesus calls His twelve apostles. It is
interesting to note that Jesus calls these 12 out from a larger
group of disciples. John Martin describes this group of disciples in contrast to apostles.

Before Jesus chose the 12 disciples, He spent an entire
night in prayer. Jesus had a large number of disciples
and from those He picked 12 who were to be close to
Him. These were specifically called apostles (*aposto-
lous*) as opposed to the term disciples (*mathētas*). Disciples were followers, but apostles were those sent out
as messengers with delegated authority (cf. "apostles"
in 9:10; 17:5; 22:14; 24:10).[16]

From these texts, we can establish that Jesus had not only
twelve disciples/apostles but also a larger group of disciples, at
one time totaling up to seventy-two. These individuals includ-

ed both men and women. This group went on mission for Jesus, supported Him in His ministry, and were taught on a more personal level than the crowds (John 6:60-67); Jesus taught a larger group of disciples than the twelve. Ultimately, many of these disciples would turn away from Him).

The Role of the Teacher

The teacher is to be a guide shepherding the learners through the amazing journey of spiritual growth. The perfect example of masterful teaching is the Lord Jesus Christ. Throughout the Gospels we see the powerful methods utilized by Christ to share truth. Whether the medium was parable, story, miracle, command, or exposition, Jesus revealed that He understood His audience and the appropriate method to apply truth to their life. Christ was the profound example of an initiator of learning.

Furthermore, the teacher serves as a living example of the truth that is taught. As the teacher grows in his own walk with the Lord, he reveals the triumphs and struggles that result in a life pleasing to God. Demonstrating the importance of this living example, the Apostle Paul exhorts his readers to follow him as he follows Christ (1 Cor. 11:1). Through consistent growth on the part of the teacher, the student is challenged intellectually, socially, and spiritually as he learns from his teacher's example.

Not only is the teacher a guide and example, but he or she also serves as an authority within the classroom. The teacher selects, sequences, and organizes the knowledge that will be dispensed to the student. Instead of an environment in which the student directs the learning, this author holds the viewpoint that the teacher is the one who directs the learning process and the knowledge that is disseminated. The teacher must also hold a high level of expectation for his/her students.

Discipleship in the Teaching Ministry

Through the teaching ministries of a church, discipleship occurs to a smaller audience than the preaching ministry. In this avenue of discipleship, topics and biblical texts can be examined in a more personal and applicable way. The teacher can interact with the students and engage them in the lesson. Active learning techniques can be applied to the lesson so that individual learners become participants in the study.[17] By doing so, these individuals appropriate the biblical truths in a more practical way. Teaching lessons can be hand-tooled to focus on specific issues that the class is currently encountering as well as answering specific questions asked by individuals or by the group.

In addition, these ministry groups can serve as a vehicle for both mission and fellowship. I have witnessed many churches using these groups ranging from 20–100 as missional teams reaching into the spheres of influence of the individual members of the group. By doing so, they resemble the pattern described in Luke 10:1–20. In my church, our adult teaching ministry groups are labeled Adult Bible Fellowships (ABFs). Many of these ABFs function as both missional groups and fellowship groups with activities designed for the group itself to foster community.

The teaching ministry provides an excellent step in the discipleship process in it that helps people connect through community, relate to the teaching on a more personal level, and practice mission in a group context with support.

The Small Group Ministry

When churches describe discipleship groups, small groups are often what comes to mind. This group is an essential component in the discipleship process. In small groups, individuals experience accountability, support, and closeness with others, and they are challenged to grow spiritually on a very personal level.

Jesus and the Twelve

Jesus spent most of His teaching ministry focused on the small group context. This smaller group setting was the primary vehicle that Jesus used to teach disciples. In their book on discipleship, Harrington and Absalom highlight the importance of the small group context in disciple making and leadership development.

> *Jesus used the small group as his forum for leadership development.* Jesus called the future leaders of the church into a small group relationship with himself. He gave his life to these men as he trained and discipled them and then entrusted the future of his whole ministry to them. Jesus gave both this relational model and his message of salvation that the world would come to believe. It was with the Twelve that Jesus taught his most important lessons:
>
> - What true greatness means (Mark 9:35)
> - What love looks like (John 13:1–38)
> - How to spread the gospel in word and deed (Luke 10; Mark 9) …

Clearly, discipleship in the Personal Context is vital for those who want to follow Jesus and make disciples like Jesus did. The Personal Context is the perfect environment for asking questions and applying the transformative power of the gospel to individual life.[18]

The authors summarize Jesus' small group vision well by highlighting the importance of individual connection in a more personal setting.

The Role of the Small Group Leader

One of the most prevalent trends for discipleship in recent decades has been the practice of small groups. Many churches have restructured their Christian education plans based on the certain belief that small groups will effectively promote the spiritual growth of adult men and women within the congregation. Small groups are so widespread that they may now be seen as the basic unit of the church community. The common assumption in many churches is that the small group educational strategy has greater potential to produce Christian maturity than do large group class formats or even one-on-one mentoring.[19]

There are many benefits to utilizing small groups in a discipleship setting. One benefit is the impact of relational learning on an individual. A widespread emphasis in small group ministry is the importance of establishing close relationships to enhance community among group members. Small group models have the potential for healthy ideals and positive implications. Many people grow best in a community, not in isolation. Education involves real-life issues rather than the mere mastery of facts. In our post-Christian society where so many have experienced brokenness, abuse, and addiction, believers often can find love, healing, and acceptance in the body of Christ through small groups.[20]

A second benefit is that small groups can function as an instrument for change. Small groups are beneficial in that they provide collective aid to produce individual change within the members of the group. A third benefit is that small groups allow for open discussion. A significant advantage of a learning group is the collective gathering of greater resources than individuals have on their own. Through discussion, the group shares resources. In addition, participants in group discussion are often stimulated to succeed by the presence of others and change their individual attitudes and behavior.[21]

Though there are many benefits to small groups, there are some cautions that need to be observed. It has been observed that there are group problems that arise with some regularity. [22] 1) Groups can occasionally be hurtful. 2) A group can be sincere, concerned, and sensitive, but also completely self-centered. 3) A common problem in groups is the existence of a small power clique within the group. 4) Groups often fail when they do not meet the needs of their members. 5) Groups often run into problems with relationships between members. These problems often can immobilize the group.

The following are several suggestions for leaders of small groups. Though this list was designed for groups in educational settings, the list can easily be applied to small groups in the discipleship context: 1) stress the importance of the task, 2) enhance the esteem of individuals through recognition or by delegating responsibility, 3) emphasize the shared interests of all group members, 4) help members accept the overall group purposes, 5) encourage reflection and inquiry in discussion by affirmation of member discovery, 6) plan programs with meticulous care, and 7) encourage interaction among members.[23]

Discipleship in the Small Group Ministry

In the discipleship context, when dealing with the teaching of Scripture, it is important that a small group is aware of and guards against relativism. Often, Bible study within a small group begins with the question, "What does this passage mean to you?" This question is harmful in that it confuses the *meaning* of a passage with the *significance* of the passage. The meaning of a text of Scripture never changes, but the application and significance of that text to the life of a believer is flexible. E. D. Hirsch states the following: "Meaning is that which is represented by a text; it is what the author meant.... Significance, on the other hand, names a relationship between that meaning and a person, or a conception, or a situation, or indeed anything imaginable."[24] It is important to safeguard the small group from digressing into potential negative outcomes through relativism.

Though cautions need to be observed in a small group discipleship setting, there are many benefits of a small group teaching model.

- Individuals can experience accountability with the group.
- Individuals can be challenged spiritually on a very practical level.
- Individuals can ask personal questions in a safe and trusted environment.
- Practical applications can be made on a personal level.
- Individual prayer requests can be shared with the group.
- Spiritual support can be given on a practical and personal level.

These are just a few of the advantages of small groups in discipleship. With the proper safeguards in place, participation in a small group can have a significant impact upon individuals in the discipleship process.

The Mentoring Ministry (Coaching/ One-on-One Mentoring)

The most personal of the ministry avenues in discipleship is mentoring. Mentoring occurs in one-on-one relationships or between a mentor and a very small group (2–4 individuals). In this discipleship relationship, intimate accountability and instruction takes place. This is the deepest level of church discipleship in the lives of believers.

Jesus and the Inner Circle and with Individuals

The clearest expression of this mentoring relationship is found with Jesus and the inner circle and with specific individuals. As discussed earlier, Jesus had a group of twelve apostles that were selected from a larger group of disciples. Within that group of twelve, there is a recognized inner circle of three individuals that Jesus taught at a deeper level. This inner circle was comprised of Peter, James, and John. These three experienced a deeper level of teaching and mentorship. The following are various passages in the Gospels where Jesus specifically and intimately instructed the inner circle.

- Mark 1:29–31—Jesus healed Peter's mother-in-law with Peter, James, and John present.

- Mark 5:37–43—Jesus raised Jairus's daughter from the dead. The passage states that He only allowed the inner circle to accompany Him.

- Mark 9:2–13—On the Mount of Transfiguration, Jesus took only Peter, James, and John with Him.

- Matthew 26:37–38—Jesus invites the inner circle to come with Him apart from the Twelve to pray with Him in the Garden of Gethsemane.

Jesus separated out this group of three at times for special instruction, prayer, and mentorship.

In addition to the example of Jesus, we read throughout Scripture of numerous examples of individuals modeling the mentoring method of discipleship. Mentoring took place among Hebrew priests (Eli and Samuel), prophets (Elijah and Elisha), leaders (Moses and Joshua), kings (David and Solomon), spiritual leaders (Paul and Aquila and Priscilla, Aquila and Priscilla and Apollos), and pastors (Paul and Timothy).

The Role of the Mentor

Throughout history, the role of the mentor to apprentice is a unique and powerful relationship. From a secular perspective, Daniel Levinson, in a study of adult male development, places great emphasis on mentoring relationships. He describes the functions of a mentor:

> He may act as a teacher to enhance the young man's skills and intellectual development. Serving as sponsor, he may use his influence to facilitate the young man's entry and advancement. He may be a host and guide, welcoming the initiate into a new occupational and social world and acquainting him with its values, customs, resources and cast of characters. Through his own virtues, achievements and way of living, the mentor may be an exemplar that the protégé can admire and seek to emulate. He may provide counsel and moral support in times of stress. The mentor has another function, and this is developmentally the most crucial one: to support and facilitate the realization of the Dream.[25]

Levinson found that the mentoring relationship was extremely important in development of an adult male. From this list of ways that a mentor impacts the development of an adult male, we readily see how many of these characteristics equally apply in biblical mentorship within a discipleship relationship.

The mentor serves as an example for a disciple to follow. Much like Paul stated in 1 Cor 11:1, "Be imitators of me, just as I also am of Christ," mentors serve as a model to those that learn from them. The mentor also serves as an instructor applying truths from Scripture in a personal and meaningful way.

Discipleship in the Mentoring Ministry

The most intimate avenue of discipleship within the church is found in mentoring relationships. It is through mentoring relationships that true vulnerability, accountability, openness, and personal transformation occur in the life of a disciple. Scriptural truths come alive as one individual instructs another to appropriate biblical teaching on a practical and specific area of life. Through mentorship, sins can be discussed freely and confidentially. Deficiencies in one's spiritual walk can be addressed specifically. Applications can be made on a particular level. Biblical truths can be exemplified through individual participation. Mission can be experienced with personal assistance and guidance. For these reasons, individual mentorship is the goal and deepest level of discipleship in the church.

Chapter 7
Personal Avenues of Discipleship

IN THE LAST CHAPTER, we examined the avenues of discipleship for the church. Oftentimes, believers are content to stop the discipleship process at the church. An inaccurate assumption is made by these individuals that the church provides every avenue for discipleship. However, God calls us to be fervent in discipleship outside the walls of the church building. We are to practice discipleship in our homes and in our personal lives. This chapter focuses on personal avenues of discipleship and challenges us to take the process of discipleship out from the confines of the church and into our homes and personal devotional life.

Discipleship in the Home

One of the most neglected battlegrounds for discipleship is within our homes. Oftentimes, churches will have activities, events, retreats, children and teen programs, and parents assume that their children are being educated by the church. As I have been involved in pastoral ministry for many years, I have heard the statement: "I'm leaving it to the church to educate my child in the Scriptures." Nothing could be further from what is taught in Scripture, and nothing could be more heart-breaking to the church leadership than to hear that discipleship is not taking place within the home.

We are responsible for the Scriptural training of our families. Yes, the church can assist and provide our families with well-rounded opportunities for service and missions as well as provide a strengthening of the Scriptures that we are teaching in our homes. However, we as the parents in the home are held responsible by God for the scriptural development and teaching of the Scriptures to our children.

A critical passage in Scripture that describes the discipleship that is to take place within the home is found in Deuteronomy 6:4–9.

> Hear, O Israel! The LORD is our God, the LORD is one! You shall love the LORD your God with all your heart and with all your soul and with all your might. These words, which I am commanding you today, shall be on your heart. You shall teach them diligently to your sons and shall talk of them when you sit in your house and when you walk by the way and when you lie down and when you rise up. You shall bind them as a sign on your hand and they shall be as frontals on your forehead. You shall write them on the doorposts of your house and on your gates.

Several important aspects of this passage need to be observed as we seek to understand what Moses is telling parents in Deuteronomy 6.

- Parents, specifically fathers, were primarily responsible for instructing their children in the knowledge and commands of God.

- The teaching was to take place all the time as parents modeled biblical instruction before their children.

- Moses uses the literary tool of a "merism" to demonstrate God's specific command to the parents of the children of Israel. A "merism" provides two extremes and implies everything in between (i.e., "when you sit in your house and when you walk by the way." A parent does not only teach when they sit in the house or walk on the road but also in numerous additional opportunities throughout the day). In this example parents are commanded to repeatedly teach the Word of God to their children.

- The emphasis is on the repeated action of teaching God's commands and words so that the next generation will continue in obedience to the Lord.

- The curriculum that is to be spoken is God's Word. The book of Deuteronomy was Moses' opportunity to convey to the new generation of Israelites the importance of obeying God's commands as he rehearsed the Law of God with them.

In Deuteronomy 6, Moses specifically instructs parents that *they* are responsible to continue the instruction that has been placed before them. Parents are commanded to repeatedly teach and speak the words of God to their children in every action, place, and time. Discipleship is a primary function of parents to their children. Though pastors, teachers, and church leaders assist and disciple the next generation, Moses was clear in his instruction that the primary role of discipling the next generation was the responsibility of parents. Bible reading, Bible study, and prayer should be happening on a regular basis in our homes. With the inundation of secular philosophies that are bombarding the minds of our children, it is imperative we as parents teach our children the truths of Scripture.

Discipleship as a Pattern of Life

Developing an Intimate Relationship with God

We all understand the importance of maintaining a deep relationship with our spouse or children. Think about it: how do we foster a healthy relationship with our spouses? Among several appropriate answers to that question, one major answer would be through proper and regular communication. One cannot have a healthy marriage without proper communication.

In a broader sense, one cannot maintain healthy relationships with others without proper communication. Communication's greatest illusion may be that it is easily achieved. We must intentionally work at proper communication skills. What components are found within good communication skills? Obviously, we need to listen (this is not a marriage counseling book, but often this is a major problem in many marriages). Listening is an art. We must be actively involved in the process of listening to learn what the other is trying to say to us. This leads to the next major component in good communication: we need to speak. These two components are essential in communication.

The same is true in our relationship with God. To have an intimate and close relationship with our Savior, we must regularly communicate with Him. Without regular communication, how can we expect to know Him? To have a healthy relationship with God, we must listen to Him as He speaks to us (through Bible reading) and we must speak with Him (through prayer).

Regular Bible Reading

What will happen to me when I study the Bible? As we observed earlier, 2 Timothy 3:17 provides us with an answer to this question: "so that the man of God may be adequate, equipped for every good work." First, regularly reading God's Word will get me into shape spiritually so that I am equipped to do all that God calls me to do.

Why are so many Christians spiritually flabby? Because they don't read and study God's Word. The Bible helps believers build spiritual muscles (1 Tim 4:7). Why are so many Christians spiritually anemic? Because they do not regularly eat from the meat of God's Word. I cannot know how God expects me to live if I don't read His Word. I cannot know the promises that God has for me if I don't read His Word. It's a simple concept. Through God's Word, He speaks to me. I cannot know what He has for me without reading the Bible. I cannot be equipped to live righteously in this world if I am not regularly reading and studying the Bible.

Second, regularly reading God's Word will bring me spiritual success. Joshua 1:8 tells us how we can have success spiritually. "This book of the law shall not depart from your mouth, but you shall meditate on it day and night, so that you may be careful to do according to all that is written in it; for then you will make your way prosperous, and then you will have success." God commanded Joshua to meditate and study His Word. If Joshua would be careful to learn and obey the truths of God's Word, he would have prosperity and success in his future service to God. Marten Wouldstra comments on this important text: "Daily meditation on the Book, and a strict observance of its gracious provisions for a life in covenant fellowship with the Lord, will mean a happy achievement of life's goal and prosperity."[1]

However, we need to be cautious to understand the success that God is speaking about. David Howard comments on what success looks like from a biblical standpoint.

> Many Christians read these and other passages as guarantees that all Christians will (or should!) succeed in every venture they undertake and that they will prosper financially if they are truly following God. Christians who do not succeed, or who are not financially well off, are condemned as living in some persistent sin or lacking in proper faith.
>
> Much could be said in response, but here we will make only three points. First, the message of the Book of Job points in precisely the opposite direction as that argued by these Christians. That is, Job was stripped of his financial wealth for reasons that had nothing to do with any lack of faith or obedience. Job's wealth was restored again at the end of the book, but he came to a position of peace with God and acceptance of God's will in his life before his wealth was restored (Job 42:5–6). This was because he had now had a firsthand encounter with God, whereas previously his knowledge of God had been primarily secondhand.
>
> Second, the Book of Proverbs, which contains many statements about wealth and prosperity, nevertheless is clear about a balanced view of wealth.
>
> Third, the two words we find here in our passage in Joshua (1:7–8) speaking of prosperity and success are almost never used in the Old Testament to speak of financial success. Rather, they speak of succeeding in life's proper endeavors. This happens when people's lives are focused entirely on God and obedience to him. The focus of people's endeavors is not to be prosperity and success but rather holiness and obedience.[2]

Success in God's eyes may not always be success from an earthly perspective! If Joshua valued and studied God's Word, he would be successful in God's eyes. At the end of the day, being successful in God's eyes is what should motivate us! God is the ultimate Judge and the goal should be pleasing Him.

> *Discipleship in any form must be rooted in the Word.*

Third, regularly reading God's Word will reveal how precious the Bible is to life. Notice what the Bible says about how important God's Word should be to our lives.

Psalm 19:7–11

> The law of the LORD is perfect, restoring the soul; The testimony of the LORD is sure, making wise the simple. The precepts of the LORD are right, rejoicing the heart; The commandment of the LORD is pure, enlightening the eyes. The fear of the LORD is clean, enduring forever; The judgments of the LORD are true; they are righteous altogether. They are more desirable than gold, yes, than much fine gold; Sweeter also than honey and the drippings of the honeycomb. Moreover, by them Your servant is warned; In keeping them there is great reward.

Psalm 119:10–11

> With all my heart I have sought You; Do not let me wander from Your commandments. Your word I have treasured in my heart, That I may not sin against You.

Psalm 119:105

> Your word is a lamp to my feet And a light to my path.

Matthew 4:4

> But He answered and said, "It is written, 'man shall not live on bread alone, but on every word that proceeds out of the mouth of God.'"

Romans 15:4

> For whatever was written in earlier times was written for our instruction, so that through perseverance and the encouragement of the Scriptures we might have hope.

Is God's Word precious to you? Are you regularly spending time reading and studying the Bible? The first component of a healthy relationship with God is regular Bible reading.

Consistent Prayer Life

The second component to a healthy relationship with God is a consistent prayer life. It has been said that prayer is a privilege. But do we treat prayer as a privilege? How often do we, as believers, turn to God as a last resort? When a personal issue arises in your life, examine your process for getting help. For many of us the list looks a lot like this: we call our best friend, then we talk to our spouse, then we turn to self-help books, then we worry about the problem endlessly until we cannot stand it anymore, then—when all else fails—we pray. With our mouths we say prayer is a privilege, but our actions often prove otherwise.

Talking to our God should be second nature, but many Christians consider prayer to be a challenge. Why is prayer so difficult for us?

- We get easily distracted.
- We are talking to someone we cannot see or audibly hear from in return.

- We feel inadequate talking to the God of the universe.
- We don't know what God's response will be to our request.
- We struggle to express our hurt into words.
- We are not disciplined enough to pray regularly, so we feel guilty.
- Our need does not seem important enough to present to God.

Prayer is a wonderful benefit for the believer. We can talk to God. The God who created and rules the universe wants our fellowship. The Almighty and all-powerful God wants to help us. The God of all comfort is waiting to supply us with His grace and peace in our times of need. God wants us to talk with Him! Prayer is truly a privilege, and we need to make it a regular part of our lives (1 Thess 5:17).

If prayer is going to become a priority for us and something we practice on a regular basis, then we need to remember several important truths about prayer. First, it is important to remember the need for prayer. Throughout Scripture, God commands us to pray. It is interesting that the verbs in these verses are not merely suggestions or encouragements but rather commands. God commands us to pray to Him: "*pray* for those who persecute you" (Matt 5:44); "With all prayer and petition *pray* at all times in the Spirit" (Eph 6:18); "but in everything by prayer and supplication with thanksgiving *let* your requests be made known to God" (Phil 4:6); "*Devote* yourselves to prayer" (Col 4:2); "*pray* without ceasing; in everything *give thanks*; for this is God's will for you in Christ Jesus" (1 Thess 5:17–18) (the italicized words are imperatives or commands). Not only does God command us to pray, but Jesus (God Himself) provides the example for the need of prayer: "But Jesus Himself would often slip away to the wilderness and pray" (Luke 5:16); "It was at this time that He went off to the mountain to pray, and He spent the whole night in prayer to God" (Luke 6:12). The early church also realized the need for prayer and devoted themselves to it as they sought to serve God (Acts 2:42).

Second, it is important to remember the privilege of prayer. Scripture reveals to us how much God loves and cares for us (John 3:16; 15:13). Because He loves us so dearly, He calls us to take the anxieties of our lives and place them on Himself (1 Peter 5:7). He has the power to help, carry, and change the anxieties we carry with us like baggage through life. He implores (commands) us to take our cares and cast them on Him. The idea is to throw them on God, and far enough away where we cannot get them back. What a privilege of prayer! We can take all the burdens, cares, anxieties, fears, etc. and give them to our Savior because He cares that deeply for us. What a privilege! I don't have to face the difficulties of life alone, and neither do you. Our God will shoulder the load if we turn it over to Him through prayer. You may be saying, "Well, I don't think God cares about the small things in my life." We forget that God cares about and knows about every aspect of our lives (Matt 6:25–34). He urges us to come boldly before Him with our requests (Heb 4:16).

Third, it is important to remember the benefits of prayer. As we pray to our heavenly Father, God hears and desires to answer our prayers (Matt 21:22). Not only does He desire to answer, but the Holy Spirit aids us in our prayers as well (Rom 8:26). He helps us offer our prayers to God. So, what good can my prayers accomplish? James in his letter reminds us of the impact and benefit that our prayers can bring. In James 5:16, he states, "The effective prayer of a righteous man can accomplish much." As the pastor of my own church, Stephen

Davey, preached this text, he explained what this important verse revealed. James is saying, "the petition of an ordinary believer is powerful. Young or old in years, young or old in faith, your prayers are heard!"[3] Our prayers are energized by God, and they accomplish great good. What a benefit of prayer! I can pray to a God who desires to listen, who aids me in my prayers to Him, and who energizes my prayers so that they are powerful to accomplish good.

Scripture provides us with the need, the privilege, and the benefits of our prayers. God desires for you to talk with Him. Instead of running to everyone else, losing sleep at night, or wringing your hands in despair, take your concerns to your Heavenly Father. He desires to listen. But I would be remiss if I did not remind us that God is not a genie for us to make demands. He is a God who demands our respect and praise. Our prayers may be of various lengths and content, from the simple "Lord, please help me" to a lengthy deliberate prayer where we include important aspects of communion with God. Jesus in the "Lord's prayer" (Matt 6:9–13) provides a pattern for deliberate prayer. Prayer is a vital tool that we can use to praise, thank, and worship God for who He is, and what He has done for us. It is also through prayer that we ask for forgiveness and aid as we seek to serve and obey our Wonderful Savior, aligning our will to His perfect plan. Prayer is a wonderful privilege for us as believers.

A key ingredient in discipleship is our communication with God. Through the Bible, God speaks to us. Through prayer, we speak to God. For growth to happen within the life of a believer, prayer needs to become a priority for his or her spiritual walk. The question is: Is prayer a priority for you?

Chapter 8
Discipleship Today and Tomorrow

Though many individual churches are intentional and faithful in making disciples of Christ, collectively the church has major issues that must be addressed if we are going to produce Christ followers. This book seeks to expose some of the issues we are facing in discipleship, to provide a proper understanding of what a disciple looks like, and to describe how discipleship takes place in the church, in our homes, and in our personal lives. The goal of this book is to help the reader understand biblical discipleship and apply it in today's context (discipleship today).

But what about tomorrow? How do we successfully impact the next generation for Christ? How do we train up future disciples to follow Christ in a hostile world? What steps need to be taken now to impact discipleship tomorrow? I want to challenge you as a disciple maker. If you fill one of the roles in the categories below, please take to heart my challenges as you strive to disciple others for Christ.

Challenge to Pastors/Church Leaders

It is critical that you as a church leader are intentional about discipleship. Matthew 28:19–20 is not a suggestion. It is the great commission. You are commanded to make disciples. That process of disciple-making must be intentional, systematic, and designed specifically for the growth of believers. You cannot just "happen" into discipleship. Discipleship must be planned and appropriated to the lives of believers.

Do you as a church leader have an intentional program in place to educate believers in their walk with Christ? Have you thought through the practice of discipleship for your church? Do you have a philosophy of discipleship? Is your teaching content intentionally designed or do you simply pick random series/studies to teach through from the pulpit or in the classroom? We must be intentional in our discipleship process both in its design and in the content that we teach.

Is your discipleship program comprehensive in *scope*? Do you have a prescribed *sequence* of instruction to prepare believers to study the scriptures, apply those truths to their lives, and answer the difficult questions they are facing in today's world?

In addition, remember that discipleship programs are for all believers in the church. Are you truly discipling children and teens within the church? How about new believers? Are you designing curriculum to help them grow in Christ?

I think that if we are honest we will admit that most of our attention in the preaching/teaching ministry is designed for the mature believer. While it is important for mature believers to continue to grow in their walk with Christ, you must be intentional in helping newer believers progress in the growth (sanctification) process.

Challenge to Discipleship Teachers/Mentors

One of the most important roles within the church is that of the teacher and mentor. Through your instruction of Scripture, a believer is challenged in their walk with Christ. A teacher and mentor can apply the truths of Scripture in a specific and practical way. In addition, you serve as a guide or example to follow. That is a big responsibility!

Are you spending adequate time in preparation to deliver the truths of God's Word to other believers? Are you teaching the Bible or your own opinions or thoughts? It is easy to get distracted or off track in teaching sessions or mentoring meetings. It is critical that you teach the Bible! The tool that God uses to change a life is His Word. Therefore, you must be teaching the Bible. Please remember to be careful not to digress into empty discussions and mundane conversation. These teaching/mentoring times are so valuable as you examine the truths of God's Word and bring them to life for believers as they apply them to their individual lives.

Challenge to Parents

One of the areas that Satan targets the most is the home. Without strong homes, the church and the nation suffer. Satan is targeting your children. That is not a comforting thought for us as parents, but it is true. Satan does not want the next generation to impact the world for Christ. It is critically important that you as a parent teach and model the truths of Scripture to your children. They look up to you! They learn how to love, live the truths of Scripture, and serve their God by watching your example.

Are you displaying a love for God in your home? Do you personally spend time in Bible study and prayer? Do you teach the truths of Scripture not just in word but also in deed? Are you setting the example of Christian living in your home? I hope that you realize the impact your life and example have on your children. You must live in such a way that your actions and words point your children to Jesus Christ!

Challenge to You as a Follower of Christ

The following challenges are for all of us! If you are a believer in and follower of Christ, these challenges are for you. In chapters 3 and 4, discipleship principles were gleaned from Matthew 28:19–20, Luke 6:40, Luke 14:26–27, John 15:7–8, Romans 12:1–2, and 2 Timothy 2:2. Are you practicing these discipleship principles? Is your life reflecting Christlikeness to the world? As you re-examine these discipleship principles, ask yourself the following questions for each principle.

Discipleship Principles

Make Disciples (Lifetime Learners)

Am I actively involved in both evangelism and discipleship?

Have I neglected Jesus' primary command
to the church, to disciple others?

Do I actively seek to impact the next generation for Christ?

Resemble the Master in All Areas of Life

Am I seeking to replicate the example of the Master?

Am I living my life focused on being spiritually, morally,
and ethically different from the world around me?

Be Singular in Your Allegiance to Christ No Matter the Cost

Am I allowing the world to pull my allegiance away from Christ?

Am I consumed by selfish desires, or is
Christ my single devotion?

Is my comfort my utmost priority?

Am I willing to sacrifice my comforts to follow Christ?

Are there things or individuals that I place before Christ?

Am I willing to lay aside my desires to follow the Savior?

Do I love others more than myself, and God above all?

Display Specific Characteristics as a Disciple of Christ

Am I characterized by an intimate relationship with Jesus Christ?

Do I have a passion for the Word of God?

Do I regularly read and study God's Word?

Do I or those I disciple understand what meditation is?

Am I seeking to be biblically literate—
understanding God's truths for my life?

Do I demonstrate a consistent prayer life?

Do I have a heart for ministry and service?

Display a Proper Mindset in Relationship to This World

Do I remain distinct from the world?

Do I view my life as a sacrifice, or am I
determined to make my life easy?

Would others view me as living blamelessly in this present world?

You Are to Replicate Yourself into the Lives of Others

Am I faithfully reproducing myself
spiritually in the lives of others?

Am I teaching the truths of Scripture to my children,
new believers, younger men, younger women, etc.?

Discipleship Today and Tomorrow

My prayer for you is that God would use these principles found within this book to challenge your heart and spiritual walk. Whether you are a church leader, discipleship mentor, parent in the home, or a disciple in a church, discipleship is a mandate for our lives. It is not an option for us believers (Matt 28:19-20). Our world and our churches are in desperate need of disciples of Jesus Christ. The world needs to see men and women who will live differently and reveal a life dedicated to Jesus Christ. Are you faithfully following Him? Are you growing in your walk with Him? Are you discipling others (2 Tim 2:2)? May God richly bless you as you obediently follow His commission to you, "make disciples of all the nations."

Endnotes

Chapter 1

[1] Arizona Christian University, "Inaugural CRC Study: Dangerously Low Percentage of Americans Hold Biblical Worldview," 24 March 2020, https://www.arizonachristian.edu/2020/03/24/inaugural-crc-study-dangerously-low-percentage-of-americans-hold-biblical-worldview/.

[2] Ibid.

[3] Ibid.

[4] Ibid.

[5] Ibid.

[6] John S. Dickerson, *The Great Evangelical Recession: 6 Factors That Will Crash the American Church … and How to Prepare* (Grand Rapids, MI: Baker Books, 2013), 22.

[7] Ibid., 22–23.

[8] Ibid., 98.

[9] David Kinnaman, *You Lost Me: Why Young Christians are Leaving Church … and Rethinking Faith* (Grand Rapids, MI: Baker Books, 2011), 22.

[10] Ibid., 23.

[11] The Barna Group, "Barna Studies the Research, Offers a Year-in-Review Perspective," *The Barna Group—Barna Update*, n.d.,

http://www.barna.org/barna-update/article/12-faithspirituality/
325-barna-studies-the-research-offers-a-year-in-review-perspective.

[12] George H. Guthrie, "Will we rise to biblical literacy?", 31 January 2011, https://www.baptistpress.com/resource-library/news/first-person-george-h-guthrie-will-we-rise-to-biblical-literacy/

[13] The Barna Group, *Barna Studies the Research*, 2009.

[14] David Roach, "Bible Reading Drops During Social Distancing," *Christianity Today*, 22 July 2020, https://www.christianitytoday.com/news/2020/july/state-of-bible-reading-coronavirus-barna-abs.html

[15] Stephen R. Prothero, *Religious Literacy: What Every American Needs to Know—and Doesn't* (New York, NY: HarperOne, 2008), 7.

[16] The Barna Group, "Six Megathemes Emerge from Barna Group Research in 2010," n.d., https://www.barna.org/barna-update/culture/462-six-megath-emesemerge-from-2010.

[17] Stephen Marlin, "Barna Research Group: Megatheme: Biblical Illiteracy!", n.d., http://hopeforbrazil.com/wordpress/barna-research-group-megatheme-bib-lical-illiteracy/.

[18] Albert Mohler, "The Scandal of Biblical Illiteracy: It's Our Problem," *Albert Mohler*, 14 October 2005, http://www.albertmohler.com/2005/10/14/the-scandal-of-biblical-illiteracy-its-our-problem/.

[19] The Barna Group, *Barna Studies the Research*, 2009.

[20] Craig S. Keener, *The Gospel of Matthew: A Socio-Rhetorical Commentary (Grand Rapids, MI: Eerdmans, 2009),* 14.

[21] James M. Boice, *Christ's Call to Discipleship* (Chicago, IL: Moody Press, 1986), 13.

[22] George Barna, *Growing True Disciples: New Strategies for Producing Genuine Followers of Christ (Colorado Springs, CO: WaterBrook Press, 2001),* 6.

[23] Ibid., 6–7.

[24] Eric Geiger, Michael Kelley, and Philip Nation, *Transformational Discipleship: How People Really Grow* (Nashville, TN: B&H Publishing Group, 2012), 10.

[25] Ibid., 16.

Chapter 2

[1] Bauer, Walter, William F. Arndt, Wilbur Gingrich, and Fredrick W. Danker, *A Greek-English Lexicon of the New Testament and Other Early Christian Literature* (2d ed.; Chicago, IL: University of Chicago Press, 1979), s.v. μαθητης, 486.

[2] Richard N. Longenecker, *Patterns of Discipleship in the New Testament* (Grand Rapids, MI: Eerdmans, 1996), 2.

[3] Michael J. Wilkins, *Discipleship in the Ancient World and Matthew's Gospel* (2d ed.; Grand Rapids, MI: Baker Books, 1995), 45–51.

[4] G. H. Trever, "Disciple" in *The International Standard Bible Encyclopedia: Vol 2* (ed. James Orr; Peabody, MA: Hendrickson Publishers, 1984), 851.

[5] Gerhard Kittel, *Theological Dictionary of the New Testament: Vol. 4*, edited and translated by G.W. Bromiley (Grand Rapids, MI: Eerdmans, 1967), 391–461.

[6] Michael Wilkins expounds that in Classical Greek, the word was used to describe three main groups:

1) In a general sense with reference to someone who is learning from another (i.e., apprentice).

2) In a technical sense referencing an individual who studies under a particular teacher (i.e., student).

3) In a restricted sense referring specifically to a Sophist pupil.

Michael J. Wilkins, "Disciples," in *Dictionary of Jesus and the Gospels: A Compendium of Contemporary Biblical Scholarship* (ed. Joel B. Green, Scot McKnight, and I. Howard Marshall; Downers Grove, IL: InterVarsity, 1992), 176–182.

[7] David L. Turner, *Matthew* (BECNT; Grand Rapids, MI: Baker Academic, 2008), 689–90.

[8] Donald A. Carson, "Matthew," in *The Expositor's Bible Commentary: Matthew, Mark, Luke* (ed. Frank E. Gæbelein; vol. 8; Grand Rapids, MI: Zondervan, 1984), 595–96.

[9] Donald A. Hagner, *Matthew 14–28* (WBC 33B; Nashville, TN: Thomas Nelson, 1995), 887.

[10] Jori Finkel, "A Rembrandt Identity Crisis," *New York Times*, 4 December 2009, https://www.nytimes.com/2009/12/06/arts/design /06rembrandt.html.

[11] Michael J. Wilkins, *Following the Master* (Grand Rapids, MI: Zondervan, 1992), 77–78.

[12] Barna, *Growing True Disciples, 18.*

[13] Wilkins, *Following the Master, 40.*

[14] Brad J. Waggoner, *The Shape of Faith to Come: Spiritual Formation and the Future of Discipleship* (Nashville, TN: B&H Publishing Group, 2008), 14.

[15] Wilkins, *Following the Master*, 40.

[16] Barna, *Growing True Disciples, 18.*

Chapter 3

[1] Ulrich Luz, *Matthew 21–28: A Commentary on Matthew 21–28* (ed. Helmut Koester; trans. James E. Crouch; Hermeneia; Minneapolis, MN: Fortress Press, 2005), 625–26.

[2] Grant R. Osborne, *Matthew* (ZECNT 1; Grand Rapids, MI: Zondervan, 2010), 1080.

[3] Louis A. Barbieri Jr., "Matthew," in *The Bible Knowledge Commentary: An Exposition of the Scriptures* (ed. J. F. Walvoord and R. B. Zuck; vol. 2; Wheaton, IL: Victor Books, 1985), 94.

[4] Craig L. Blomberg, *Matthew* (NAC 22; Nashville, TN: B&H Publishing Group, 1992), 431.

[5] Daniel B. Wallace, *Greek Grammar Beyond the Basics: An Exegetical Syntax of the New Testament* (Grand Rapids, MI: Zondervan, 1996), 640.

[6] Osborne, *Matthew*, 1080.

[7] Blomberg, *Matthew*, 431.

[8] Osborne, *Matthew*, 1080.

[9] Turner, *Matthew*, 689.

[10] R. T. France, *The Gospel of Matthew* (NICNT; Grand Rapids, MI: Eerdmans, 2007), 1115.

[11] Wallace, *Greek Grammar Beyond the Basics*, 645.

[12] Osborne, *Matthew*, 1081.

[13] Barbieri, *The Bible Knowledge Commentary*, 93–94.

[14] Gerhard Kittel, Gerhard Friedrich, and Geoffrey William Bromiley, *Theological Dictionary of the New Testament, Abridged in One Volume* (Grand Rapids, MI: W.B. Eerdmans, 1985), 92.

[15] Keener, *The Gospel of Matthew*, 720.

[16] Turner, *Matthew*, 690.

[17] Blomberg, Matthew, 431.

[18] Turner, *Matthew*, 690.

[19] John Nolland, *The Gospel of Matthew: A Commentary on the Greek Text* (NIGTC; Grand Rapids, MI: Eerdmans, 2005), 1270.

[20] Nolland, *The Gospel of Matthew*, 1271.

[21] David Thomas, *The Gospel of St. Matthew: An Expository and Homiletic Commentary* (Grand Rapids, MI: Baker Book House, 1956), 559.

[22] Blomberg, *Matthew*, 432.

[23] Keener, *The Gospel of Matthew*, 720.

[24] Blomberg, *Matthew*, 431.

[25] I. Howard Marshall, *The Gospel of Luke: A Commentary on the Greek Text* (NIGTC 3; Grand Rapids, MI: Eerdmans, 1978), 269.

[26] Darrell L. Bock, *Luke* (BECNT 1; Grand Rapids, MI: Baker Books, 1996), 612.

[27] Ibid.

[28] David E. Garland, *Luke* (ZECNT 3; Grand Rapids, MI: Zondervan, 2011), 284.

[29] Ceslas Spicq, *Theological Lexicon of the New Testament, Vol. 2* (trans. and ed. James D. Earnest; Peabody, MA: Hendrickson, 1994), 274.

[30] Garland, *Luke*, 284.

[31] Robert J. Marzano, Debra Pickering, and Jane E. Pollock, *Classroom Instruction That Works: Research-Based Strategies for Increasing Student Achievement* (Alexandria, VA: Association for Supervision and Curriculum Development, 2001), 3.

[32] S. Paul Wright, Sandra P. Horn, and William L. Sanders, "Teacher and Classroom Context Effects on Student Achievement: Implications for Teacher Evaluation," *Journal of Personnel Evaluation in Education* 11 (1997), 63.

[33] John Nolland, *Luke 1-9:20* (WBC 35A; Dallas, TX: Word Books, 1989), 307.

[34] Thomas W. Hudgins, *Luke 6:40 and the Theme of Likeness Education in the New Testament* (Eugene, OR: Wipf & Stock, 2014), 43.

Endnotes

James Limburg, *Psalms* (Louisville, KY: Westminster John Knox, 2000), 81.

36 Hudgins, *Luke 6:40*, 45.

37 François Bovon, *Luke 1: A Commentary on the Gospel of Luke 1:1–9:50* (ed. Helmut Koester; trans. Christine M. Thomas; Hermeneia; Minneapolis, MN: Fortress Press, 2002), 249.

38 Ibid.

39 Hudgins, *Luke 6:40*, 42.

40 Bovon, *Luke 1*, 387.

41 Simon J. Kistemaker, *The Parables of Jesus* (Grand Rapids, MI: Baker Book House, 1980), 203.

42 Marshall, *The Gospel of Luke*, 591.

43 François Bovon, *Luke 2: A Commentary on the Gospel of Luke 9:51–19:27* (ed. Helmut Koester; trans. Donald S. Deer; Hermeneia; Minneapolis, MN: Fortress Press, 2013), 389.

44 Marshall, *The Gospel of Luke*, 591.

45 Bovon, *Luke 2*, 386.

46 Marshall, *The Gospel of Luke*, 592.

47 Garland, *Luke*, 600. Garland lists the following references as examples of this Semitic interpretation as to preference to one over another: Gen 29:30–33 (speaking of Jacob, "he loved Rachel more than Leah"); Deut 21:15–17; Mal 1:2–3; Luke 16:13; and Rom 9:13.

48 Marshall, *The Gospel of Luke*, 592.

49 Bock, *Luke*, 1284–85.

50 Bovon, *Luke 2*, 387.

51 Ibid.

52 Bock, *Luke*, 1284.

53 Ibid., 1285.

54 Joel B. Green, *The Gospel of Luke* (NICNT; Grand Rapids, MI: Eerdmans, 1997), 565.

55 Bock, *Luke*, 1285.

[56] Garland, *Luke*, 601.

[57] Bovon, *Luke 2*, 386.

[58] Bock, *Luke*, 1286–87.

[59] Garland, *Luke*, 601.

[60] Bovon, *Luke 2*, 389.

[61] Vassilios Tzaferis, "Crucifixion—The Archaeological Evidence," *BAR* 11 Jan/Feb (1985), 48–50.

[62] Martin Hengel, *Crucifixion in the Ancient World and the Folly of the Message of the Cross* (trans. John Bowden; Philadelphia, PA: Fortress Press, 1977), 22. Hengel's work is an extensive revelation of the horrors of crucifixion. Hengel provides an examination of the historical evidence regarding crucifixion including the history of crucifixion, the various methods utilized in crucifixion, as well as the horror of the crucifixion process. After studying his book, the reader truly understands that ancient crucifixion is indeed "obscene."

Chapter 4

[1] Henry G. Liddell and Robert Scott, *A Greek-English Lexicon. 8th ed.* (New York, NY: American Book Company, 1882), 941.

[2] Kittel, *Theological Dictionary of the New Testament: Vol.4*, 574.

[3] Joel B. Green, Jeannine K. Brown, and Nicholas Perrin, *Dictionary of Jesus and the Gospels. Second ed.* (Downers Grove, IL: InterVarsity Press, 2013), 1. The term *meno* is used multiple times in the NT corpus.

Over half of the 118 NT occurrences of the word meno ("to abide" or "to remain") are found in the Johannine corpus (40x in John's Gospel and 27x in the Johannine Epistles, compared with three references in Matthew, two in Mark and seven in Luke). Believers' need to "abide" in Christ, in turn, is presented as part of John's trinitarian mission theology, according to which Jesus' followers are taken up into the love, unity, and mission of Father, Son, and Spirit and charged to continue Jesus' mission until he returns.

As believers "abide" in Christ, they reflect the intimate relationship between the Trinity.

[4] Ibid., 2.

[5] Gerald L. Borchert, *John 12–21* (NAC 25B; Nashville, TN: Broadman & Holman, 2002), 145.

[6] Andreas J. Köstenberger, *John* (BECNT; Grand Rapids, MI: Baker Academic, 2004), 454 and D. A. Carson, *The Gospel According to John* (PNTC; Grand Rapids, MI: Eerdmans, 1990), 517.

[7] Köstenberger, *John*, 454.

[8] Carson, *The Gospel According to John*, 517.

[9] Raymond E. Brown, *The Gospel According to John (XIII–XXI)* (2d ed.; AB 29A; New York, NY: Doubleday, 1970), 662.

[10] Craig S. Keener, *The Gospel of John: A Commentary* (vol. 2; Peabody, MA: Hendrickson, 2003), 1000. Keener explains this idea of *meno* involving more than just "dwell" but also "remain."

The demand for perseverance plays a central role in this pericope. In this context, μενω signifies not only "dwell" (as in 14:10, 17) but "remain" (both are legitimate components of the term's semantic range functioning in this context). John 8:31 warns initial believers that they must "abide" in his "word" so that they may be his "disciples" in truth. The passage alludes back to all the major concepts of 8:31, expanding them in connection with the image of the vine: they must "abide" (15:4–7); his "word" has cleansed them (15:3) and his "words" should abide in them (15:7); those who abide bear fruit and hence prove to be his "disciples" (15:8).

The term implies that this "remaining" should be evident in our daily actions as disciples of Christ.

[11] E. M. Bounds, *The Weapon of Prayer* (New Kensington, PA: Whitaker House, 1996), 8. Bounds describes the importance of prayer in the life of a believer:

In dealing with mankind, nothing is more important to God than prayer. Prayer is likewise of great importance to people. Failure to pray is failure in all of life. It is failure of duty, service, and spiritual progress.... We must pray to God if love for God is to exist. Faith and hope and patience and all strong, beautiful, vital forces of piety are withered and dead in a prayerless life. An individual believer's life, his personal salvation, and his personal Christian graces have their being, bloom, and fruit in prayer. All this and much more can be said about how prayer is necessary to the life and piety of the individual. But prayer has a larger sphere, a loftier inspiration, a higher duty. Prayer concerns God.

According to Bounds, prayer is an essential dynamic of the Christian's life and is important to God.

[12] Leon Morris, *The Gospel According to John* (rev. ed.; NICNT; Grand Rapids, MI: Eerdmans, 1995), 562.

[13] Carson, *The Gospel According to John*, 517–18.

[14] Morris, *The Gospel According to John*, 597.

[15] Keener, *The Gospel of John*, 997. Keener expounds on the interpretation of the "fruit" described in John 15:7–8.

In John's larger usage, one might suppose the fruit of Christian witness (4:36; 12:24), but the immediate context, which bears more weight than John's usage elsewhere when the usage is so rare (two texts), suggests moral fruit. This is the most common sense of the metaphor in other traditions about Jesus and John the Baptist with which this Gospel's first audience may have been familiar (Matt 3:8, 10; 7:16–20; 12:33; Luke 3:8–9; 6:43–44; 13:6–9; probably Mark 11:14; 12:2); other early Christian writers also develop it (Gal 5:22; Phil 1:11; Eph 5:9; Col 1:10; Heb 12:11; Jas 3:18; Jude 12).

According to Keener, the idea of "fruit" is moral fruit that is displayed in the life of a believer.

[16] Douglas J. Moo, *The Epistle to the Romans* (NICNT; Grand Rapids, MI: Eerdmans, 1996), 748.

[17] Robert H. Mounce, *Romans* (NAC 27; Nashville, TN: Broadman & Holman, 1995), 231.

[18] Charles E. B. Cranfield, *A Critical and Exegetical Commentary on the Epistle to the Romans: Volume 2* (ICC; Edinburgh: T&T Clark, 2000), 597.

[19] Mounce, *Romans*, 231.

[20] Marvin R. Vincent, *Word Studies in the New Testament: Volume III* (Peabody, MA: Hendrickson, 1991), 153.

[21] Josephus, *The Works of Josephus,* 109. *Ant 4:113.*

[22] John MacArthur, *Romans 9–16* (MacArthur New Testament Commentary; Chicago, IL: Moody Press, 1994), 142. "As members of God's present 'holy priesthood' (1 Pet. 2:5), Christians are here exhorted to perform what is essentially a priestly act of worship. Because the verb is in the imperative, the exhortation carries the weight of a command."

[23] John 1:29—"The next day he saw Jesus coming to him and said, 'Behold, the Lamb of God who takes away the sin of the world!'"

[24] MacArthur, *Romans 9–16,* 145.

[25] Moo, *The Epistle to the Romans*, 750. Moo expounds on this understanding of sacrifice:

At the same time, the NT use of cultic language has an important salvation-historical and polemical function, claiming for Christianity the fulfillment of those institutions so central to the OT and to Judaism. Christians offer no bloody sacrifice on an altar; but they offer "spiritual sacrifices" (1 Pet. 2:5), such as the "sacrifice of praise to God, which is the fruit of lips that acknowledge his name" (Heb. 13:15). In Rom. 15:16, Paul describes his own missionary work in cultic terms (see also Phil. 2:17; and note Phil. 3:3 and 4:18).

New Testament believers do not offer the Old Testament bloody sacrifices to God, but rather they are involved in spiritual sacrifices or acts of service to God.

[26] F. F. Bruce, *Romans* (TNTC 6; Grand Rapids, MI: Eerdmans, 1993), 213.

[27] Moo, *The Epistle to the Romans*, 751.

[28] MacArthur, *Romans 9–16*, 146.

[29] Colin G. Kruse, *Paul's Letter to the Romans* (PNTC; Grand Rapids, MI: Eerdmans, 2012), 461.

[30] N. T. Wright, *The New Interpreter's Bible, Vol. X: Letter to the Romans* (Nashville, TN: Abingdon Press, 2002), 704.

[31] Genesis 4:3–7 describes the sacrifices that Adam and Eve and subsequently their offspring (Cain and Abel) were to offer to God.

So it came about in the course of time that Cain brought an offering to the LORD of the fruit of the ground. Abel, on his part also brought of the firstlings of his flock and of their fat portions. And the LORD had regard for Abel and for his offering; but for Cain and for his offering He had no regard. So Cain became very angry and his countenance fell. Then the LORD said to Cain, "Why are you angry? And why has your countenance fallen? If you do well, will not your countenance be lifted up? And if you do not do well, sin is crouching at the door; and its desire is for you, but you must master it."

God demanded an animal sacrifice from Cain and Abel. When Cain brought his own sacrifice to the altar, God did not accept the offering. Sacrifices were an essential part of the Old Testament Jewish religious system.

[32] Moo, *The Epistle to the Romans*, 750–51. "'Body' can, of course, refer to the physical body as such, and the metaphorical associations with sacrifice make it an appropriate choice here. But Paul probably intends to refer to the entire person, with special emphasis on that person's interaction with the world."

Endnotes

33 Kruse, *Paul's Letter to the Romans*, 462.

34 Moo, *The Epistle to the Romans*, 751.

35 Mounce, *Romans*, 231.

36 Moo, *The Epistle to the Romans*, 751.

37 Mounce, *Romans*, 231. Mounce continues by describing the spiritual sacrifice that believers are to make to God.

This expression has been variously translated as "spiritual service, reasonable worship, rational service," and so on. Perhaps the best paraphrase is that of Knox, "This is the worship due from you as rational creatures." In view of God's acts of mercy it is entirely fitting that we commit ourselves without reservation to him. To teach that accepting the free gift of God's grace does not necessarily involve a moral obligation on our part is a heresy of gigantic proportions. The popular cliché "He is Lord of all or not Lord at all" is absolutely right.

This worship that we as believers give to God is a necessary outpouring when disciples understand that God is King of all.

38 Mounce, *Romans*, 232. Mounce describes the world system and its negative influence on the life of believers.

As citizens of heaven (Phil 3:20) we are to "set [our] minds on things above, not on earthly things" (Col 3:2). Paul reminded the Galatians that the present age is evil (Gal 1:4). It cannot, and must not, serve as a model for Christian living. Its values and goals are antithetical to growth in holiness. The church should stand out from the world as a demonstration of God's intention for the human race. To be culturally identified with the world is to place the church at risk. Believers are to be salt and light (Matt 5:13–14), purifying and enlightening contemporary culture.

According to Mounce, instead of being "conformed" to the wicked worldly system, disciples are to live in a distinctly different way than the world proposes.

39 John Phillips, *Exploring Romans* (Grand Rapids, MI: Kregel Publications, 1969), 186.

40 Moo, *The Epistle to the Romans*, 755.

41 Ibid., 756.

[42] Mounce, *Romans*, 232.

[43] Moo, *The Epistle to the Romans*, 756.

[44] Ibid., 756–57.

[45] Mounce, *Romans*, 232.

[46] Ibid., 232–33. Mounce describes the nature and characteristics of a mind that is set on the things of God.

By nature our thoughts tend to dwell on the ephemeral. But that which passes quickly is normally inconsequential. As Paul said in another place, "What is seen is temporary, but what is unseen is eternal" (2 Cor 4:18). The mind renewed enables us to discern the will of God. Released from the control of the world around us, we can come to know what God has in mind for us. We will find that his will is "good, pleasing and perfect." It is good because it brings about moral and spiritual growth. It is pleasing to God because it is an expression of his nature. It is perfect in that no one could possibly improve on what God desires to happen.

A renewed mind has a radically different perspective than the world's system. It can discern God's will for one's life and ultimately is pleasing to God because it reveals sensitivity to God's leading.

[47] Thomas D. Lea and Hayne P. Griffin, *1, 2 Timothy, Titus* (NAC 34; Nashville, TN: Broadman Press, 1992), 201.

[48] Gordon D. Fee, *1 and 2 Timothy, Titus* (NIBC 13; Peabody, MA: Hendrickson, 1988), 240.

[49] Lea and Griffin, *1, 2 Timothy, Titus*, 201. "The command 'entrust' (παρατίθημι) comes from the same word family as the noun 'deposit' (παραθηκη) of 1:14. The clear reference to the gospel in that verse makes it likely that Paul here conveys the same idea."

[50] Martin Dibelius and Hans Conzelmann, *The Pastoral Epistles: A Commentary on the Pastoral Epistles* (ed. Helmut Koester; trans. Philip Buttolph and Adela Yarbro; Hermeneia; Philadelphia, PA: Fortress Press, 1972), 108.

[51] George W. Knight, *The Pastoral Epistles: A Commentary on the Greek Text* (NIGTC; Grand Rapids, MI: Eerdmans, 1992), 390. Knight describes what Paul has entrusted to Timothy.

Endnotes

Paul refers to this message with the indefinite plural relative pro-
noun α, which is appropriately rendered by the broad and indefinite
terms "what" (RSV) or "the things [which]" (NIV, NASB) and which
includes all his teaching (cf. 1:13–14). He has made explicit this sense
of the authority and permanent significance of his words on several
earlier occasions (cf. 1 Thess 2:13). He speaks of his teaching as "tra-
dition(s)" (παραδοσις) received from him and to be held and followed
by Christians (2 Thess 2:15; 3:6–7) and commends the Corinthians
for holding firmly to the "traditions" just as he delivered them (1 Cor
11:2).

Paul has entrusted "traditions" to Timothy which includes the
teachings of Paul.

52 John MacArthur, *2 Timothy* (MacArthur New Testament Commentary; Chicago, IL: Moody Press, 1995), 40.

53 Risto Saarinen, *The Pastoral Epistles with Philemon & Jude*
(BTCB; Grand Rapids, MI: Brazos Press, 2008), 134.

54 Donald A. Carson, Douglas J. Moo, and Leon Morris, An Introduction to the New Testament (2d ed.; Grand Rapids, MI: Zondervan,
2005), 581.

There is a "given" about the Christian faith; it is something inher-
ited from the very beginning of God's action for our salvation, and it
is to be passed on as long as this world lasts. Paul is not arguing that
believers should be insensitive to currents of thought and action in
the world about them, nor is he saying that the Christian is a kind of
antiquarian, interested in antiquity for its own sake. He is saying that
there is that about the essence of the Christian faith that is not open to
negotiation. God has said and done certain things, and Christians must
stand by those things whatever the cost.

It is essential that believers guard those sacred truths of the Christian faith no matter what the cost.

55 William Barclay, *The Letters to Timothy, Titus, and Philemon*
(Philadelphia, PA: Westminster, 1957), 182.

56 MacArthur, *2 Timothy*, 41. "That which he was to carefully
guard (1:14: cf. 1 Tim. 6:20) he also was to carefully teach. The truth
Paul is talking about here is beyond the basic gospel message of salva-

tion, which is to be preached to all who will hear. He is rather talking about the careful, systematic training of church leaders who will teach and disciple other believers in the fullness of God's Word."

[57] Philip H. Towner, *The Letters to Timothy and Titus* (NICNT; Grand Rapids, Eerdmans, 2006), 491.

[58] William D. Mounce, *Pastoral Epistles* (WBC 46; Waco, TX: Word Books, 2000), 504.

[59] Knight, *The Pastoral Epistles*, 392.

[60] Lea and Griffin, *1, 2 Timothy, Titus*, 201.

Chapter 5

[1] Lea and Griffin, *1, 2 Timothy, Titus*, 235.

[2] Mounce, *Pastoral Epistles*, 566.

[3] Knight, *Pastoral Epistles*, 444.

[4] Ibid., 446.

[5] Lea and Griffin, *1, 2 Timothy, Titus*, 236.

[6] Philip H. Towner, *The Letters to Timothy and Titus* (NICNT; Grand Rapids, MI: Eerdmans, 2006), 585.

[7] R. C. H. Lenski, *The Interpretation of St. Paul's Epistles to the Colossians, to the Thessalonians, to Timothy, to Titus, and to Philemon* (Columbus, OH: Wartburg, 1946), 847.

[8] Lea and Griffin, *1, 2 Timothy, Titus*, 237-238.

[9] Ibid., 237.

[10] Fee, *1 and 2 Timothy, Titus*, 280.

[11] John B. Polhill, *Acts* (NAC 26; Nashville, TN: Broadman & Holman, 1992), 273.

[12] F. F. Bruce, *The Book of the Acts* (rev. ed.; NICNT; Grand Rapids, MI: Eerdmans, 1988), 228.

[13] Peter T. O'Brien, *The Letter to the Ephesians* (PNTC; Grand Rapids, MI: Eerdmans, 1999), 300–1.

[14] Marvin R. Vincent, *Word Studies in the New Testament: Vol. 3* (McLean, VA: MacDonald Publishing Company, 1985), 390.

[15] John MacArthur, *Ephesians* (MacArthur New Testament Commentary; Chicago, IL: Moody Press, 1986), 155. MacArthur explains that the pastors themselves cannot do all the work of the ministry.

No pastor, or even a large group of pastors, can do everything a church needs to do. No matter how gifted, talented, and dedicated a pastor may be, the work to be done where he is called to minister will always vastly exceed his time and abilities. His purpose in God's plan is not to try to meet all those needs himself but to equip the people given into his care to meet those needs (cf. v. 16, where this idea is emphasized).

In contrast to the pastors doing all the work in a church, these leaders are to train the believers of the church to help carry out the work of the ministry.

16 Ibid.

17 Clinton E. Arnold, *Ephesians* (ZECNT 10; Grand Rapids, MI: Zondervan, 2010), 262.

18 Ibid., 262–63.

19 Harold W. Hoehner, *Ephesians: An Exegetical Commentary* (Grand Rapids, MI: Baker Academic, 2002), 551.

20 BDAG, s.v. τέλειος, 809.

21 Hoehner, *Ephesians*, 554.

22 BDAG, s.v. νήπιος, 537.

23 Hoehner, *Ephesians*, 560.

24 F. F. Bruce, *The Epistles to the Colossians, to Philemon, and to the Ephesians* (NICNT; Grand Rapids, MI: Eerdmans, 1984), 351. Bruce describes this spiritual infancy as:

[A]n immaturity which is culpable when sufficient time has passed for those so described to have grown out of infancy. Paul tells the Corinthian Christians that, for all their cultivation of "knowledge," he could not address them as spiritual men and women but as "infants in Christ," still needing to be fed with milk rather than solid food (1 Cor. 3: 1–2). Infants are defenseless, unable to protect themselves; in the spiritual life they are an easy prey for false teachers and others who would like to lead them astray from the true path. Like ships at sea without adequate means of steering, they are tossed about by the waves and carried this way and that according to the prevailing wind. Maturity brings with it the capacity to evaluate various forms of teaching, to accept what is true and reject what is false.

Spiritual infants, according to Bruce, lack the discernment to adequately determine spiritual decisions and truths.

25 Hoehner, *Ephesians*, 561.

26 Ibid.

27 O'Brien, *Ephesians*, 308–9.

[28] Ibid., 309. O'Brien describes the source of this false teaching that is counteracting the teaching of the church leaders.

Behind this dangerous and misleading teaching by which immature believers are tossed to and fro are deceitful people who seek to manipulate them by evil trickery. Paul's language is graphic, if not forthright. The false teaching which causes so much strife is promoted by the cunning of men. Cunning literally refers to dice-playing and comes to be used metaphorically of a trickery that results from craftiness, while the qualifier of men (as in Col. 2:8, 22) depicts it as human—that, and nothing more—and therefore opposed to Christ and his teaching.

These false teachers were evil in that they through cunning words sought to derail the lives of believers.

[29] Hoehner, *Ephesians*, 561–62.

Chapter 6

[1] Bobby Harrington and Alex Absalom, *Discipleship That Fits: The Five Kinds of Relationships God Uses to Help Us Grow* (Grand Rapids, MI: Zondervan, 2016), 61. For several years prior to the printing of this book, I have taught in my discipleship courses at multiple seminaries that we must view discipleship from a holistic perspective. Harrington and Absalom have come the closest to the perspective that I teach. They separate discipleship into five contexts for the church. I will be describing four primary ministry avenues. Some of our perspectives will overlap.

[2] Osborne, *Matthew*, 165.

[3] Louis A. Barbieri Jr., "Matthew," in *The Bible Knowledge Commentary: An Exposition of the Scriptures* (ed. J. F. Walvoord and R. B. Zuck; vol. 2; Wheaton, IL: Victor Books, 1985), 28.

[4] Edwin A. Blum, "John," in *The Bible Knowledge Commentary: An Exposition of the Scriptures* (ed. J. F. Walvoord and R. B. Zuck; vol. 2; Wheaton, IL: Victor Books, 1985), 293–94.

[5] Howard Hendricks, *The Christian Educator's Handbook on Teaching* (Grand Rapids, MI: Baker Books, 1988), 13.

[6] Richard A. Batey, ed, *New Testament Issues* (New York, NY: Harper and Row, 1970), 71.

[7] Hendricks, *The Christian Educator's Handbook on Teaching*, 26.

[8] Ibid.

[9] Ronald B. Allen, *Lord of Song: The Messiah Revealed in the Psalms* (Portland, OR: Multnomah Press, 1985), 57-58.

[10] Hendricks, *The Christian Educator's Handbook on Teaching*, 27.

[11] Ibid., 27–28.

[12] Harrington and Absalom, *Discipleship That Fits*, 76.

[13] Ibid., 77.

[14] Ibid., 93.

[15] Garland, *Luke*, 425.

Endnotes

[16] John A. Martin, "Luke," in *The Bible Knowledge Commentary: An Exposition of the Scriptures* (ed. J. F. Walvoord and R. B. Zuck; vol. 2; Wheaton, IL: Victor Books, 1985), 219.

[17] Iowa State University, "226 Active Learning Techniques," n.d., www.celt.iastate.edu/wp-content/uploads/2017/03/CELT226active-learningtechniques.pdf. These techniques provide an example of how the teacher can engage students in the lesson.

[18] Harrington and Absalom, *Discipleship that Fits*, 133.

[19] Mary Rynsburger and Mark A. Lamport, "All the Rage: How Small Groups Are Really Educating Christian Adults Part 1: Assessing Small Group Ministry Practice: A Review of the Literature," *Christian Education Journal* 5 (2008): 116–17.

[20] Rynsburger and Lamport, "All the Rage," 117

[21] Thorrel B. Fest, Barbara Schindler Jones, R. Victor Harnack, *Group Discussion: Theory and Technique* (Hoboken, NJ: Prentice-Hall, 1977), 13–18.

[22] The following list comes (with modification) from Clyde Reid, *Groups Alive—Church Alive: The Effective Use of Small Groups in the Local Church* (New York, NY: Harper & Row, 1969), 102–4.

[23] Halbert E. Gulley, *Discussion, Conference, and Group Process* (2d ed.; New York, NY: Holt Rinehart Winston, 1968), 233–36.

[24] E. D. Hirsch Jr., *Validity in Interpretation* (New Haven, CT: Yale University Press, 1967), 8.

[25] Daniel J. Levinson, *The Seasons of a Man's Life* (New York, NY: Knopf, 1978), 98–99.

Chapter 7

[1] Marten H. Woudstra, *The Book of Joshua* (NICOT; Grand Rapids, MI: Eerdmans, 1981), 63.

[2] David M. Howard Jr., *Joshua* (NAC 5; Nashville, TN: Broadman & Holman, 1998), 87.

[3] Stephen Davey, *James: Expository Commentary on the New Testament* (Cary, NC: Charity House Publishers, 2018), 361.

References

Allen, Ronald B. *Lord of Song: The Messiah Revealed in the Psalms*. Portland, OR: Multnomah Press, 1985.

Arizona Christian University. "Inaugural CRC Study: Dangerously Low Percentage of Americans Hold Biblical Worldview." 24 March 2020. https://www.arizonachristian.edu/2020/03/24/inaugural-crc-study-dangerously-low-percentage-of-americans-hold-biblical-worldview/.

Arnold, Clinton E. *Ephesians*. Zondervan Exegetical Commentary on the New Testament 10. Grand Rapids, MI: Zondervan, 2010.

Barbieri Jr., Louis A. "Matthew." Pages 13-94 in vol. 2 of *The Bible Knowledge Commentary: An Exposition of the Scriptures*. Edited by J. F. Walvoord and R. B. Zuck. 2 vols. Wheaton, IL: Victor Books, 1985.

Barclay, William. *The Letters to Timothy, Titus and Philemon*. Philadelphia, PA: Westminster, 1957.

Barna, George. *Growing True Disciples: New Strategies for Producing Genuine Followers of Christ*. Colorado Springs, CO: WaterBrook Press, 2001.

Batey, Richard A., ed. *New Testament Issues*. New York, NY: Harper and Row, 1970.

Bauer, Walter, William F. Arndt, Wilbur Gingrich, and Fredrick W. Danker. *A Greek-English Lexicon of the New Testament and Other Early Christian Literature*. 2nd ed. Chicago, IL: University of Chicago Press, 1979.

Blomberg, Craig L. *Matthew*. New American Commentary 22. Nashville, TN: B&H Publishing Group, 1992.

Blum, Edwin A. "John." Pages 267-348 in vol. 2 of *The Bible Knowledge Commentary: An Exposition of the Scriptures*. Edited by J. F. Walvoord and R. B. Zuck. 2 vols. Wheaton, IL: Victor Books, 1985.

Bock, Darrell L. *Luke*. Baker Exegetical Commentary on the New Testament 1 (1:1-9:50). Grand Rapids, MI: Baker Books, 1994.

Borchert, Gerald L. *John 1-11*. New American Commentary 25A. Nashville, TN: Broadman & Holman, 1996.

———. *John 12–21*. New American Commentary 25B. Nashville, TN: Broadman & Holman, 2002.

Bounds, E. M. *The Weapon of Prayer*. New Kensington, PA: Whitaker House, 1996.

Bovon, François. *Luke 1: A Commentary on the Gospel of Luke 1:1-9:50*. Edited by Helmut Koester. Translated by Christine M. Thomas. Hermeneia. Minneapolis, MN: Fortress Press, 2002.

———. *Luke 2: A Commentary on the Gospel of Luke 9:51-19:27*. Edited by Helmut Koester. Translated by Donald

S. Deer. Hermeneia. Minneapolis, MN: Fortress Press, 2013.

Boice, James M. *Christ's Call to Discipleship.* Chicago, IL: Moody Press, 1986.

Brown, Raymond E. *The Gospel According to John (XIII–XXI).* 2d ed. Anchor Bible 29A. Garden City, NY: Doubleday, 1966.

Bruce, F. F. *The Book of the Acts.* Rev. ed. New International Commentary on the New Testament. Grand Rapids, MI: Eerdmans, 1988.

_____. *The Epistles to the Colossians, to Philemon, and to the Ephesians.* New International Commentary on the New Testament. Grand Rapids, MI: Eerdmans, 1984.

_____. *Romans.* Tyndale New Testament Commentaries 6. Grand Rapids, MI: Eerdmans, 1993.

Carson, D. A. "Matthew." Pages 1-599 in *The Expositor's Bible Commentary: Matthew, Mark, Luke.* Edited by Frank E. Gaebelein. Vol. 8. Grand Rapids, MI: Zondervan, 1984.

_____. *The Gospel According to John.* Pillar New Testament Commentary. Grand Rapids, MI: Eerdmans, 1990.

Carson, Donald A., Douglas J. Moo, and Leon Morris. *An Introduction to the New Testament.* 2d ed. Grand Rapids, MI: Zondervan, 2005.

Cranfield, Charles E. B. *A Critical and Exegetical Commentary on the Epistle to the Romans: Volume 2.* International Critical Commentary. Edinburgh: T&T Clark, 2000.

Davey, Stephen. *James: Expository Commentary on the New Testament.* Cary, NC: Charity House Publishers, 2018.

Dibelius, Martin and Hans Conzelmann. *The Pastoral Epistles: A Commentary on the Pastoral Epistles.* Edited by Helmut Koester. Translated by Philip Buttolph and Adela Yarbro. Hermeneia. Philadelphia, PA: Fortress Press, 1972.

Dickerson, John S. *The Great Evangelical Recession: 6 Factors That Will Crash the American Church … and How to Prepare.* Grand Rapids, MI: Baker Books, 2013.

Fee, Gordon D. *1 and 2 Timothy, Titus.* New International Bible Commentary 13. Peabody, MA: Hendrickson, 1988.

Fest, Thorrel B., Barbara Schindler Jones, and R. Victor Harnack. *Group Discussion: Theory and Technique.* Hoboken, NJ:Prentice-Hall, 1977.

Finkel, Jori. "A Rembrandt Identity Crisis." *New York Times.* 4 December 2009. https://www.nytimes.com/2009/12/06/arts/design/06rembrandt.html.

France, R. T. *The Gospel of Matthew.* New International Commentary on the New Testament. Grand Rapids, MI: Eerdmans, 2007.

Garland, David E. *Luke.* Zondervan Exegetical Commentary on the New Testament 3. Grand Rapids, MI: Zondervan, 2011.

Geiger, Eric, Michael Kelley, and Philip Nation. *Transformational Discipleship: How People Really Grow.* Nashville, TN: B&H Publishing Group, 2012.

References

Green, Joel B. *The Gospel of Luke*. New International Commentary on the New Testament. Grand Rapids, MI: Eerdmans, 1997.

Green, Joel B., Jeannine K. Brown, and Nicholas Perrin, eds. *Dictionary of Jesus and the Gospels*. 2d ed. Downers Grove, IL: InterVarsity Press, 2013.

Gulley, Halbert E. *Discussion, Conference, and Group Process*. 2d ed. New York, NY: Holt Rinehart Winston, 1968.

Guthrie, George H. "Will we rise to biblical literacy?", 31 January 2011, https://www.baptistpress.com/resource-library/news/first-person-george-h-guthrie-will-we-rise-to-biblical-literacy/

Hagner, Donald A. *Matthew 14–28*. Word Biblical Commentary 33B. Nashville, TN: Thomas Nelson, 1995.

Harrington, Bobby and Alex Absalom. *Discipleship that Fits: The Five Kinds of Relationships God Uses to Help Us Grow*. Grand Rapids, MI: Zondervan, 2016.

Hendricks, Howard. *The Christian Educator's Handbook on Teaching*. Grand Rapids, MI: Baker Books, 1988.

Hengel, Martin. *Crucifixion in the Ancient World and the Folly of the Message of the Cross*. Translated by John Bowden. Philadelphia, PA: Fortress Press, 1977.

Hirsch, E. D. Jr. *Validity in Interpretation*. New Haven, CT: Yale University Press, 1967.

Hoehner, Harold W. *Ephesians: An Exegetical Commentary*. Grand Rapids, MI: Baker Academic, 2002.

Howard, David M. Jr. *Joshua*. New American Commentary 5. Nashville, TN: Broadman & Holman, 1998.

Hudgins, Thomas W. *Luke 6:40 and the Theme of Likeness Education in the New Testament*. Eugene, OR: Wipf & Stock, 2014.

Iowa State University. "226 Active Learning Techniques." No date. www.celt.iastate.edu/wp-content/uploads/2017/03/CELT226activelearningtechniques.pdf.

Josephus, Flavius. *The Works of Josephus: Complete and Unabridged*. New updated ed. Peabody, MA: Hendrickson Publishers, 1987.

Keener, Craig S. *The Gospel of John: A Commentary*. 2 vols. Peabody, MA: Hendrickson, 2003.

_____. *The Gospel of Matthew: A Socio-Rhetorical Commentary*. Grand Rapids, MI: Eerdmans, 2009.

Kinnaman, David. *You Lost Me: Why Young Christians are Leaving Church … and Rethinking Faith*. Grand Rapids, MI: Baker Books, 2011.

Kistemaker, Simon J. *The Parables of Jesus*. Grand Rapids, MI: Baker Book House, 1980.

Kittel, Gerhard and Gerhard Friedrich, eds. *Theological Dictionary of the New Testament*. Translated by Geoffrey W. Bromiley. 10 vols. Grand Rapids, MI: Eerdmans, 1967.

Knight, George W. *The Pastoral Epistles: A Commentary on the Greek Text*. New International Greek Testament Commentary. Grand Rapids, MI: Eerdmans, 1992.

Köstenberger, Andreas. J. *John*. Baker Exegetical Commentary on the New Testament. Grand Rapids, MI: Baker Academic, 2004.

Kruse, Colin G. *Paul's Letter to the Romans*. Pillar New Testament Commentary. Grand Rapids, MI: Eerdmans, 2012.

Lea, Thomas D. and Hayne P. Griffin. *1, 2 Timothy, Titus*. New American Commentary 34. Nashville, TN: Broadman Press, 1992.

Lenski, R. C. H. *The Interpretation of St. Paul's Epistles to the Colossians, to the Thessalonians, to Timothy, to Titus, and to Philemon*. Columbus, OH: Wartburg, 1946.

Levinson, Daniel J. *The Seasons of a Man's Life*. New York, NY: Knopf, 1978.

Liddell, Henry G. and Robert Scott. *A Greek-English Lexicon*. 8th ed. New York: American Book Company, 1882.

Limburg, James. *Psalms*. Louisville, KY: Westminster John Knox, 2000.

Longenecker, Richard N. *Patterns of Discipleship in the New Testament*. Grand Rapids, MI: Eerdmans, 1996.

Luz, Ulrich. *Matthew 21–28: A Commentary on Matthew 21–28*. Edited by Helmut Koester. Translated by James E. Crouch. Hermeneia. Minneapolis, MN: Fortress Press, 2005.

MacArthur, John. *Ephesians*. MacArthur New Testament Commentary. Chicago, IL: Moody Press, 1986.

_____. *Romans 9–16*. MacArthur New Testament Commentary. Chicago, IL: Moody Press, 1994.

_____. *2 Timothy*. MacArthur New Testament Commentary. Chicago, IL: Moody Press, 1995.

Marlin, Steve. "Barna Research Group: Megatheme: Biblical Illiteracy!". No date. http://hopeforbrazil.com/ wordpress/barna-research-group-megatheme-biblical-illiteracy/.

Marshall, I. Howard. *The Gospel of Luke: A Commentary on the Greek Text*. New International Greek Testament Commentary 3. Grand Rapids, MI: Eerdmans, 1978.

Martin, John A. "Luke." Pages 199-266 in vol. 2 of *The Bible Knowledge Commentary: An Exposition of the Scriptures*. Edited by J. F. Walvoord and R. B. Zuck. Wheaton, IL: Victor Books, 1985.

Marzano, Robert J., Debra Pickering, and Jane E. Pollock. *Classroom Instruction That Works: Research-Based Strategies for Increasing Student Achievement*. Alexandria, VA: Association for Supervision and Curriculum Development, 2001.

Mohler, Albert. "The Scandal of Biblical Illiteracy: It's Our Problem." *Albert Mohler*. 14 October 2005. http://www. albertmohler.com /2005/10/14/the-scandal-of-biblical-illiteracy-its-our-problem/.

Moo, Douglas J. *The Epistle to the Romans*. New International Commentary on the New Testament. Grand Rapids, MI: Eerdmans, 1996.

Morris, Leon. *The Gospel According to John*. Rev. ed. New International Commentary on the New Testament. Grand Rapids, MI: Eerdmans, 1995.

Mounce, Robert H. *Romans.* New American Commentary 27. Nashville, TN: Broadman & Holman, 1995.

Mounce, William D. *Pastoral Epistles.* Word Biblical Commentary 46. Waco, TX: Word Books, 2000.

Nolland, John. *Luke 1-9:20.* Word Biblical Commentary 35A. Dallas, TX: Word Books, 1989.

———. *The Gospel of Matthew: A Commentary on the Greek Text.* The New International Greek Testament Commentary. Grand Rapids, MI: Eerdmans, 2005.

O'Brien, Peter T. *The Letter to the Ephesians.* Pillar New Testament Commentary. Grand Rapids, MI: Eerdmans, 1999.

Osborne, Grant R. *Matthew.* Zondervan Exegetical Commentary on the New Testament 1. Grand Rapids, MI: Zondervan, 2010.

Phillips, John. *Exploring Romans.* Grand Rapids, MI: Kregel Publications, 1969.

Polhill, John B. *Acts.* New American Commentary 26. Nashville, TN: Broadman & Holman, 1992.

Prothero, Stephen R. *Religious Literacy: What Every American Needs to Know—and Doesn't.* New York, NY: HarperOne, 2008.

Reid, Clyde. *Groups Alive—Church Alive: The Effective Use of Small Groups in the Local Church.* New York, NY: Harper & Row, 1969.

Roach, David. "Bible Reading Drops During Social Distancing." *Christianity Today.* 22 July 2020. https://

www.christianitytoday.com/news/2020/july/state-of-bible-reading-coronavirus-barna-abs.html.

Rynsburger, Mary and Mark A. Lamport. "All the Rage: How Small Groups Are Really Educating Christian Adults Part 1: Assessing Small Group Ministry Practice: A Review of the Literature." *Christian Education Journal* 5 (2008), 116-137.

Saarinen, Risto. *The Pastoral Epistles with Philemon & Jude.* Brazos Theological Commentary on the Bible. Grand Rapids, MI: Brazos Press, 2008.

Spicq, Ceslas. *Theological Lexicon of the New Testament.* Translated and edited by James D. Ernest. 3 vols. Peabody, MA: Hendrickson, 1994.

The Barna Group. "Barna Studies the Research, Offers a Year-in-Review Perspective." *The Barna Group—Barna Update.* No date. http://www.barna.org/barna-update/article/12-faithspirituality/325-barna-studies-the-research-offers-a-year-in-review-perspective.

———. *Six Megathemes Emerge from Barna Group Research in 2010.* https://www.barna.org/barna-update/culture/462-six-megathemes-emerge-from-2010.

Thomas, David. *The Gospel of St. Matthew: An Expository and Homiletic Commentary.* Grand Rapids, MI: Baker Book House, 1956.

Towner, Philip H. *The Letters to Timothy and Titus.* New International Commentary on the New Testament. Grand Rapids, MI: Eerdmans, 2006.

Trever, G. H. "Disciple" in *The International Standard Bible Encyclopedia: Vol 2*. Ed. James Orr. Peabody, MA: Hendrickson, 1984.

Turner, David L. *Matthew*. Baker Exegetical Commentary on the New Testament. Grand Rapids, MI: Baker Academic, 2008.

Tzaferis, Vassilios. "Crucifixion—The Archaeological Evidence." *Biblical Archaeology Review* 11 Jan/Feb (1985), 44-53.

Vincent, Marvin R. *Word Studies in the New Testament: Volume III*. Peabody, MA: Hendrickson, 1985.

Waggoner, Brad J. *The Shape of Faith to Come: Spiritual Formation and the Future of Discipleship*. Nashville, TN: B&H Publishing Group, 2008.

Wallace, Daniel B. *Greek Grammar Beyond the Basics: An Exegetical Syntax of the New Testament*. Grand Rapids, MI: Zondervan, 1996.

Walvoord, John F. and Roy B. Zuck, eds. *The Bible Knowledge Commentary: New Testament*. Wheaton, IL: Victor Books, 1983.

Wilkins, Michael J. "Disciples." Pages 176–182 in *Dictionary of Jesus and the Gospels: A Compendium of Contemporary Biblical Scholarship*. Edited by Joel B. Green, Scot McKnight, and I. Howard Marshall. Downers Grove, IL: InterVarsity, 1992.

_____. *Discipleship in the Ancient World and Matthew's Gospel*. 2nd ed. Grand Rapids, MI: Baker Books, 1995.

_____. *Following the Master*. Grand Rapids, MI: Zondervan, 1992.

Woudstra, Marten H. *The Book of Joshua*. New International Commentary on the Old Testament. Grand Rapids, MI: Eerdmans, 1981.

Wright, N. T. *The New Interpreter's Bible, Vol. X: Letter to the Romans*. Nashville, TN: Abingdon Press, 2002.

Wright, S. Paul, Sandra P. Horn, and William L. Sanders. "Teacher and Classroom Context Effects on Student Achievement: Implications for Teacher Evaluation." *Journal of Personnel Evaluation in Education* 11 (1997), 57–67.

Scripture Index

Made in the USA
Columbia, SC
05 March 2024

32725002R00090